What people are saying about

# Spiritual Intelligence in Seven Steps

In Spiritual Intelligence in Seven Steps, Mark Vernon draws on the understanding of numerous individuals and cultures, weaving them into a text that leads the reader on a journey into the very heart of their self and, at the same time, to the reality that lies behind and is expressed as the world. Like the journey which his mentor, Dante, undertakes, each chapter guides us more and more deeply into the perennial understanding that lies at the foundation of our civilization.

**Rupert Spira**, Spiritual teacher, writer and studio potter

Compellingly readable, urgently important, kind, wise and scholarly. This is a manual for living and dying that begins with the usually overlooked questions: "What are we?" and "Where did we come from?" Unless we have informed answers we can't begin to say how we should behave, or what makes us thrive, or speculate on our prognosis as a species, let alone about the therapy that might avert catastrophe. Vernon's gentle, humble and powerful book needs to be widely read before it's too late for us all.

**Charles Foster**, author of Being a Human and Being a Beast

Spiritual intelligence goes well beyond what we understand as emotional intelligence. It connects us with the center of our being and our shared spiritual commons. To leave behind the false idols of our materialist imagination, we must learn to re-appreciate wonder, death, kairological time, and the glorious universal. In seven elating steps, Mark V~~~~~~~~~~~~~ can dance with the fact that spiritu~~~~ part of the human condition, and bec~~~

again. Why should we? Quite simply to avoid going extinct as a species.

**Anna Katharina Schaffner**, author of *The Art of Self-Improvement: Ten Timeless Truths*

As entertaining and passionate as it is profound, this book is a treasure trove of spiritual insight and guidance. Expertly interweaving the wisdom of mysticism, philosophy and psychology, Mark Vernon shows that spiritual awakening is the most urgent need of our time.

**Steve Taylor**, author of *The Leap and Extraordinary Awakenings*

With intellectual flair, passionate commitment and enormous scope of vision, Mark Vernon has put his finger on the spiritual impoverishment of our times, and offered a pathway to those who are seeking guidance for living soulfully in our materialist world. If we don't take this seriously and learn from both our own inner wisdom and the great philosophical and religious traditions available to us, the "decline and fall" of the twenty-first century may well be nigh. Vernon shows us how we can reflect afresh and learn what it means to live and die well – this book is a bold and challenging urge to wake up before it is too late.

**Angela Voss**, Centre for Myth, Cosmology and the Sacred

There is a widespread hunger for spiritual intelligence. In this characteristically lucid book Mark Vernon explains that it is not a proficiency achieved by an elite, but a way of perceiving things that is open to everyone. He takes his readers on a transformative journey that helps them to understand better the nature of spiritual intelligence, how it has developed, how it can be cultivated, and why it matters.

**Fraser Watts**, Visiting Professor, University of Lincoln

The world is desperately in need of the kind of spiritual intelligence which Vernon presents, based on humility, insight, compassion and, above all, joy. His attempt to talk about it in a way which is not circumscribed by specific religious belief, but rather draws upon the wisdom of all the great spiritual traditions as well as the contemporary psychology and science, is both original and immensely helpful for those who wish to cultivate these qualities in themselves.

**Jane Clark**, editor of Beshara Magazine

# Spiritual Intelligence
in Seven Steps

# Spiritual Intelligence in Seven Steps

## Mark Vernon

IFF
BOOKS

Winchester, UK
Washington, USA

JOHN HUNT PUBLISHING

First published by iff Books, 2022
iff Books is an imprint of John Hunt Publishing Ltd., No. 3 East Street, Alresford,
Hampshire SO24 9EE, UK
office@jhpbooks.com
www.johnhuntpublishing.com
www.iff-books.com

For distributor details and how to order please visit the 'Ordering' section on our website.

Text copyright: Mark Vernon 2021

ISBN: 978 1 80341 032 6
978 1 80341 033 3 (ebook)
Library of Congress Control Number: 2021952224

A CIP catalogue record for this book is available from the British Library.

Design: Matthew Greenfield

UK: Printed and bound by CPI Group (UK) Ltd, Croydon, CR0 4YY
Printed in North America by CPI GPS partners

We operate a distinctive and ethical publishing philosophy in
all areas of our business, from our global network of authors to
production and worldwide distribution.

# Contents

## Previous books

Dante's Divine Comedy: A Guide For The Spiritual Journey
Angelico Press: 2021, 978-1621387497

A Secret History of Christianity: Jesus, the Last Inkling,
and the Evolution of Consciousness
Christian Alternative: 2019, 978-1-78904-194-1

The Idler Guide To Ancient Philosophy
Idler Books: 2015, 978-0954845667

Carl Jung: How to Believe
Guardian Shorts: 2013

Love: All That Matters
Hodder Education: 2013, 978-1444156775

The Big Questions: God
Quercus: 2012, 978-1780870328

God: All That Matters
Hodder Education: 2012, 978-1444156690

How To Be An Agnostic
Palgrave Macmillan: 2011, 978-0230293212

The Good Life
Hodder Education: 2010, 978-1444112184

The Meaning of Friendship
Palgrave Macmillan: 2010, 978-0230242883

Plato's Podcasts: The Ancients' Guide to Modern Living
Oneworld: 2009, 978-1-85168-706-0

Dictionary of Beliefs and Religions (Editor-in-Chief)
Chambers Harrap: 2009, 978-0550103444

Teach Yourself: Understand Humanism
Hodder Education: 2008, 978-1444103502

Wellbeing
Acumen: 2008, 978-1844651535

42: Deep Thought on Life, the Universe, and Everything
Oneworld: 2008, 978-1851685608

What Not To Say: Finding the Right Words at Difficult Moments
Weidenfeld and Nicolson: 2007, 978-0753824320

Business: The Key Concepts
Routledge: 2002, 978-0415253246

# Acknowledgements

I am hugely indebted to many people over many years but I would particularly like to thank Nick George, who read the manuscript in various drafts, and I would also like to record my sincere thanks to Fraser Watts and Jonathan Rowson, and to the organizations they run – the International Society for Science and Religion, and Perspectiva, respectively. They supported me with finance and rich research opportunities during the writing of this book.

# Introduction

# What Is Spiritual Intelligence?

There is a type of understanding called spiritual intelligence which this book is about. It is a kind of intelligence to do with humble awareness rather than slick analysis and, when someone has it, you will think they are inspiring more than clever. It is a wonderful capacity, and a source of delight, comprehension and purpose. It is also basic to being human. But my fear is that it has become so overlooked and sidelined in the modern world that people are inclined to be sniffy about it and deny that it exists altogether.

My aim is to provide a nudge that may awaken some minds from such dogmatic slumbers, and secure spiritual intelligence more firmly in others. And fortunately, often, only a nudge is required because anyone who delights in a sunset, gasps at an insight or relaxes during an embrace – which is to say everyone who has thoughts, feelings and experiences – can only do so because the side of life that spiritual intelligence sees is operative and active. So what is it?

Spiritual intelligence is a type of perception, although unlike types of empirical perception that see, hear, touch, taste or smell, it works by spotting what is alive and implicit. It delivers the felt sense, often first glimpsed out of the corner of the mind's eye, that our experience of things is connected to a wider vitality; that what we grasp is only a fraction of what might be understood; that there is more underpinning existence which, whilst typically seeming still and quiet, appears, upon closer inspection, to be unvaryingly, universally, energetically present. To become alert to this presence is like becoming aware of light, which is not itself directly visible though simultaneously shines from all the objects it illuminates. Moreover, we can learn

1

to abide in this awareness by simple, if highly distractable, processes of recollection.

What spiritual intelligence detects is given multiple names: fire, energy, soul, spirit, ground, emptiness, meaning, power, Brahman, Tao, God, origin, source. It is a way of knowing that can sound esoteric, though it lies behind the experiences that people routinely regard as the most important in their lives. It is operative every day in homes and hospitals, as moments of compassion and connection amidst suffering and distress. It is behind the capacity to recognize and admire beautiful words and moral patterns. Dante insisted that we only have to look up to activate it, which is why the stars and sky, treetops and mountains instantly convey awe and a sense of the beyond that spiritual intelligence instinctively trusts and loves to know. With eyes attuned to see and ears to hear, echoes of the wisdom that runs through the whole of life can be detected, caught in a phrase, or made more explicit in a myth or song.

Reflecting on the notion of being tends to do the trick for me. What that brings inwardly into view is that my being rests in an existence that is independent of me and effectively boundless. I say boundless because it must be the existence of everything else that exists too: it makes no sense to say that my being is my own, private possession. As the verse of the Persian poet, Saadi, celebrates: "All human beings are members of one frame, since all, at first, from the same essence came."

Similarly, I can't think that the awareness in me and in you and in others arose independently, on as many occasions as there are conscious creatures on the planet. That would be as odd as saying my hands and your hands just happen to look the same – although at the same time, and like our hands, our awareness is our own in the ways in which it is distinctively gnarled or dexterous. Further, given that your and our being is shared, it must ripple out to connect with being itself, or to put it more correctly: our being is a ripple in being itself, like as many swirls funneling in the air or eddies twisting in the water. There is a medium in which personal consciousness occurs, which is sometimes called mind at large or pure consciousness.

Being is shared. We can be confident that the inner life we know privately within ourselves is the same in kind as the inner life that others know because the physical apparatus that correlates with inner life looks the same in all cases, and is given the name matter. As the philosopher Arthur Schopenhauer argued, we can use what it is like to be ourselves to reach towards the world at large. "We must learn to understand nature from ourselves, not ourselves from nature," he remarked.[1]

The physicist, Erwin Schrödinger, made similar points in a different way, in his book, *What is Life?* Casting an eye across Christian mysticism and the insights of Indian Vedanta, and noting that other traditions could be drawn on too, he spotted a common teaching, arising from two everyday observations. First, we never experience our consciousness in the plural. That's the fact captured in grammar when "I" is called the first person singular. Even someone with a multiple personality disorder is one personality at a time, and in a dream, we are always only one of the characters. That is doubly suggestive because the whole dream, with its many figures and details, springs from one mind – namely our mind – which leads us to Schrödinger's second observation. If the dream-I is usually unaware that there is this one mind which generates everything that it interacts with and sees, by inference our waking consciousness is the same: there is a singular, pure consciousness that is its origin too. The many minds, as diverse as there are sentient beings alive, are an aspect of the one consciousness, like the characters in a dream.

Schrödinger adds a further observation by way of confirmation. Lovers who look into each other's eyes "become aware that their thought and their joy are *numerically* one – not merely similar or identical."[2] They join together in their love, as

3

if taking a step towards the unity that links them already, which is part of why falling in love is such a powerful experience. In principle, this unity could be sensed in any encounter between human beings, which is what the mystics of the various traditions report.

## Intelligence and spiritual defined

Spiritual intelligence knows these things, implicitly or explicitly, which leads me to the phrase itself. The word "intelligence" is relatively uncontroversial, in this context meaning grasp, nous or recognition. It's worth stressing again that it is not about being erudite or smart but arises from direct intuition, though that can become highly refined. The Kalahari Bushmen of Southern Africa are intelligent in this way, with their awareness of animals and the landscape. The illiterate mystic who sees visions or angels is too, manifest as alertness to subtle things. The seer, Lorna Byrne, told me that her clairvoyance thrived because it wasn't educated out of her.

But if the meaning of the word "intelligence" in this context is uncontentious, the word "spiritual" is not. People can spend years trying to define it. For others, it is straightforwardly a turn-off, as it evokes superstition and woo. I've resorted to it partly because it is useful in signaling my conviction that there are more things in the world than can be accounted for by a materialist philosophy. Also, if spiritual seems slippery, that is only in the way that music becomes slippery when you try too tightly to define it. "What is music?" "A tune." "Beethoven didn't write tunes." "OK, it's harmony." "Beethoven loved discord." "How about, music as sounds that affect you?" "A scream does that." "I give up – only didn't someone once say, if you've gotta ask, you'll never know."

The word spiritual is also useful because if "material" means tangible stuff that can be empirically detected and measured, "spiritual" is its complement, meaning intangible stuff that is no less real, but must be apprehended or intimated. It is not the opposite of the material, but rather is the reason the material world can be so radiant. To put it the other way around, and to borrow the conclusion of Iris Murdoch: the unmistakable sign that we are spiritual creatures is that we are attracted by the brilliance of what's excellent and fine.[3] We have a love active within us that constantly searches for, and moves towards, what's good, which, when found, joins us to it and us all to the world.

## *Why now?*

I have a more specific reason that leads me to reach for the word spiritual. It is prompted by my involvement in a research group organized by the International Society for Science and Religion that is looking into these things. I feel it has become crucial to get a handle on the notion of spiritual intelligence in contrast to other kinds and, in particular, artificial intelligence. This arises from a recent twist in the story of AI. The latest advances in the development of algorithms and networks have led experts increasingly to argue that the pressing problem for humanity is not that computers will become conscious. That may or may not happen, depending upon whom you ask. The immediate concern is that AIs are already so pervasive that we are at risk of forgetting what it is to operate without their slick planning, cunning manipulation and tremendous capacity for problem-solving. The challenge is to ensure AIs benefit us more than they threaten us, which requires us to understand more fully what it means to be human. If we can be brightly aware of what it means to be conscious, as the technology continues to improve, we might have a chance of staying human in the age of the machine. We might be able to flourish if we keep recalling and remembering who we are.

Emotional intelligence isn't enough, I've concluded, partly because it looks as if AIs will increasingly be able to mimic the qualities that Daniel Goleman originally highlighted as the proficiencies of emotional intelligence. The first two competences he lists, social skills and empathy, machines can already be programmed to fake. The next two, motivation and self-regulation, machines simply don't need, as it is in their nature to keep going without hesitancy or deviation. Goleman's fifth characteristic, self-awareness, has so far eluded computers and my guess is it always will, though the danger is that it can be imitated so as to confuse humans, and is already doing so. When the supercomputer, DeepMind, perfected its capacity to play the game AlphaGo, experts described its moves as "inventive", "creative" and "intuitive". A moment's thought shows those accolades to be misnomers. As the philosopher, David Bentley Hart, is fond of pointing out, computers don't even compute, having no idea what it means to comprehend, say, that 1+1=2. They can achieve astonishing amounts without the faintest flicker of insight or, for that matter, no stirring of the capacity to find themselves impressive, as their conscious creators do. They are not even humble. Nonetheless, it will become common for computers to seem self-aware, unless we have a clearer appreciation of what that actually entails: the palpable quality called understanding, which is known in the body, the mind and the soul, and is a reflective and enjoyed facet of the reality that we all daily know. It is appreciating all that arises with an active awareness of being, which brings us back to spiritual intelligence.

If you know that you know, love that you love, delight that you delight, lament that you lament, fear that you fear, you are alert to the secret of existence that is hidden in plain sight. It is resistant to the most complete denial, such as the sceptic who goes so far as to declare that consciousness is an illusion. That makes no difference: to think consciousness is an illusion is to have a conscious understanding of consciousness, if one that is mistaken, in my view. The truly deadly thing is to fail to notice you are experiencing because you have become lost in the experience. It is this self-forgetfulness and alienation that the pervasiveness of machines can bring about, not because they have woken up, but because their impressive presence has made us fall asleep. The risk is that we become like them, not that they become like us.

What I am proposing as spiritual intelligence is related but different to the ways it has so far been defined, by the relatively few writers who have attended to it. It has been thought of as a skill that can handle values, or as an ability to discern purpose, or as a concern for ultimate issues like life and death. Experts have turned to it as a complement to emotional intelligence, rather than as the capacity that is on to another realm of the everyday, as I am suggesting. They have mooted that if emotional intelligence makes you aware of others through empathy, spiritual intelligence informs you what to do with such sympathies. But this would make spiritual intelligence a kind of know-how, and I think it is more basic. It is "know-that" – know that our plane of existence has qualities of being and consciousness and constancy and peace. That awareness will undoubtedly help with our emotional intelligence, by providing a basis from which to construe the world, pursue strivings and direct behaviors, as we will see. But spiritual intelligence as I see it is not a proficiency because it is not something to be achieved. It is a perception which you could say is born of a knack, though it only appears to elude us because it is closer to us than we are to ourselves. It invites us to turn back to the ground of our being and rebuild from there.

### For all

This is to stress that whilst spiritual intelligence can be described with sophistication and elegance, its core qualities can be known by everyone equally. There is no need to reach a certain stage of personal development to have it. I imagine that a basking lizard may enjoy it as much as a highly educated, hugely practiced, spiritual adept – though the adept will be able skillfully to discuss it. Consider Julian of Norwich's famous expression of spiritual intelligence, "all shall be well, and all shall be well, and all manner of things shall be well." Only spiritual intelligence could authentically deliver the assertion, particularly in Julian's case as she lived in fourteenth century England which has been described as the worst century ever, given its plagues, turbulence and conflicts. But what is so brilliant about her insight is that it can be understood at numerous levels. A babe in arms can know that all shall be well. An anchorite offering consolation can tell her distressed visitors that it is so too. And Julian, the theologian, can unpack how its threefold structure isn't just a rhetorical device but is an expression of a derivative insight of spiritual intelligence, which in the Christian tradition is called the Trinity. Her writings include nuanced explications of it in this way. Spiritual intelligence can seem elusive but if it is presented as elitist, it isn't spiritual intelligence.

My sense is that now is a good moment to become aware of its awareness for another reason. Many thinkers, including my colleagues at the research network, Perspectiva, believe that we live in a time of crisis that is actually a metacrisis. They mean that the challenges of the twenty-first century, from environmental collapse to social alienation, are not problems prevailing systems can fix, for all that specific policies and decisions may be able to impede pandemics and put out some of the fires. Rather, the problems have in large part been caused by the prevailing systems themselves. We live in iatrogenic times, though if a crisis is a good moment to return to basics, a metacrisis is one where that becomes a necessity. The prevailing wisdom is too much in doubt not to revisit fundamental questions, and the nature of our being is certainly one such matter.

This can sound suspiciously religious, and it is true that, in my view, ours is a moment for a conversion of sorts, though not to any one theological system or particular revelation, but to a renewal of the perception that spiritual intelligence facilitates. A sense of the nature of being is what wisdom traditions serve and seek to develop, so in a way spiritual intelligence can be said to be prior to religion. It's why there are religions, in manifold forms. Socrates was an advocate, as was Jesus, in sharply distinctive ways. Other seminal sages I'm indebted to include Lao Tzu and the Buddha, Shankara and Ibn 'Arabi, as they speak of it from their times and places.

A yearning for spiritual intelligence is also bubbling up like fresh water across the landscape of today. In more intellectual circles, the work of Iain McGilchrist comes to mind, with his case that brain lateralization is a sign that we are capable of two fundamental types of perception: one seeks to grasp and is aimed at utility, another seeks to appreciate and brings wider awareness. McGilchrist's argument is that modern Western culture has become dominated by the former, to the extent of distrusting and discounting the latter. McGilchrist goes so far as to say we have forgotten what it is to be human. I'm inclined to agree.

Popular culture is another domain in which this desire for more routinely appears. Given a compelling wrap, and an energetic plot, spiritual intelligence sells. At the heart of wildly successful movies, like *Avatar*, and some of the best-selling novels of all time, like *Harry Potter*, is a desire to know a re-enchanted world. These stories contain the myths that convey spiritual intelligence, a fact that should not be a surprise because, as the psychologist Jeff Kripal has shown, many of the greatest sci-fi and fantasy writers are shaped by spiritual experiences. They have precognitive dreams or encounters with odd entities. As a result, institutional forms of religiosity don't speak to them, or seem positively to exclude them. They are uninterested in the imperatives of church life such as boosting attendance, or treating faith as a bulwark against a perceived decline in moral values. They are interested in letting go of all

9

such securities and finding the pearl of great price. In fact, they may well better understand what, say, Jesus meant when he said, "It is expedient for you that I go away," or, "Do not cling to me!" or, "Whosoever would save their soul shall lose it." The mythological underpinnings of movies and stories contain that message remarkably often. By taking it on board, their fictional heroes hope to find eternal life. And yet, the insight is rarely preached, and even more rarely lived, by religious professionals. So people go elsewhere.

## A philosophical moment

An exception to that rule can be found in the movement I draw much from, which is the turn to the nondual approach that exists in all the major faith and wisdom traditions, often hidden away. Its significance is that it invites the individual not to think of religion as implying something they need to gain – be that forgiveness, or salvation, or assurance, or enlightenment – but instead as a recognition of what is already given, and a practice to establish cognizance of that gift within themselves.

Nondualism is sometimes called the direct path. It used to be pursued mostly by those who dedicated their entire lives to it, like nuns in convents or hermits on hills. But in the last century or so, quality teaching about the direct path has become much more accessible, in part as a response to disillusionment with traditional approaches to religion. Its time is now, and this book is my contribution to it.

Philosophically speaking, the nondual understanding would be called a type of absolute idealism. I won't be doing much detailed ontology in these pages: my approach would be called phenomenological by philosophers, on the assumption that showing not just telling is a useful way of opening minds when it comes to debate about the nature of reality; but just to say a few, indicative words about it now. Absolute idealism is the proposal that reality is, at base, not a thing, or an assembly of things, but is akin to what we call awareness, intelligence and being. It sees matter as nothing in itself, but instead as a manifestation of this mentality. This explains why, whilst it is possible to cultivate a unified awareness of being in the mind's eye, it is not possible to have a unified perception of matter, which instead appears in various forms. According to modern physics, it is, at base, quantum perturbations, called electrons and photons, that exhibit properties given names such as mass and spin. Aristotle caught the relationship between fragmented matter and ultimate mind rather well when he said that form gives being to matter – with "form" implying an active fashioning rather than a fixed template. Human beings, along with all of nature, abide in this one, unified consciousness and, I would add – in a Platonic coloring to absolute idealism – *participate* in its singular life as myriad varieties and variations of its emanating and returning vitality. Spiritual intelligence is the capacity to detect this glorious universal in the many delightful and co-creating particulars.

## *Bubbling up*

Which also explains why spiritual intelligence is found not only in overtly spiritual places. Far from it. I found it being discovered and enjoyed by participants in the improvision workshops run by Pippa Evans. Her teaching cultivates it with exercises as simple as saying "yes and" to whatever a partner in a conversation first offers. Responding in such a way invites you to attend to the space between you and the other person, from which spring all manner of unexpected, amusing and beautiful exchanges. This happens because of turning to the presence between, around, under and above us, called our shared being. (Incidentally, improvisation is often associated with comedy, which I think is significant because humor is a type of levity, the original meaning of which was a rising and expanding awareness, and the opposite of which was gravity that caused awareness to collapse or decline.)

Alternatively, there are the pilgrimages I have been on, organized by Guy Hayward. He invites modern day wayfarers to trace ancient footpaths. All they are asked to bring is sensible footwear and an intention that matters to them. "My concern". "Her work". "Our world". The simple task of walking to a hallowed destination, whilst holding a live issue in mind, invariably produces insights. I think it's because the walk opens the individual to the nascent wisdom of places that can be detected by spiritual intelligence. A pilgrim sets out with an un-AI-like mentality that is not focused on solutions and is, instead, receptive and prepared for the unexpected. Pilgrimages are another way of turning on spiritual intelligence, and an ancient one too. They were a major part of life before the Reformation and, in the ancient world, there was a school of philosophy named after the same core activity. Aristotle's followers were called the Peripatetics, probably because he taught them how body and mind can wander far when working together.

My own practice of psychotherapy can be understood in this way. The primary activity is listening and interpreting what is said so as to help what is present unfold. When the moment is what matters, more appears, catalyzed by sharing that moment – which is to say, there again is that space of intelligent being, in between and within us. There are other practices and examples. The interest in psychedelics and experiments in intentional living come to mind as additional signs that we are already living in the middle of widespread attempts at shifting and deepening our perceptions in ways that develop spiritual intelligence.

### *The seven steps*

My seven steps are a set of reflective reorientations that similarly turn the mind towards spiritual intelligence, deepen the understanding of it and, thereby, locate it more consciously in life.

The first step is to retell the origin story of human beings.

This is important because stories are like filters: they sift what we perceive of ourselves, and a lot of sifting has been going on in the latest splurge of "big history" accounts of Homo sapiens that tell the tale all the way back to our ancestors' emergence on the African savannah. What they tend to have in common is treating the spiritual element as if it were, at best, a useful delusion. I think that's wrong. We have a spiritual commons, which comes with the recognition that our life continually draws on a bigger presence. Participating in life with that awareness became the defining characteristic of the species called Homo sapiens. That is a big claim, of course, though it arises from the intuition that Homo sapiens has always been Homo spiritualis. "Spiritual hunger is part of the human condition", the leader in a British newspaper noted, which was doubly noteworthy as *The Guardian* is known for its secular rather than religious leanings.[4] It's an inkling that is backed up by innovative research seeking to understand human origins, which I discovered by participating in a research project that is looking at this question afresh. I'll discuss it as our first step.

The second step, or perceptual shift, continues this story into the annals of history, and explores how individuality and individual freedom emerged. This is important because it speaks to the complexities of how we experience ourselves since the period known as the Axial Age, and it also introduces the teachings of the adepts from that time who first articulated spiritual intelligence in ways that can still speak to us. Step two examines their wisdom.

Step three brings us to the experience of spiritual intelligence today. I've written the step as an extended meditation on what a few minutes spent recalling, forgetting and returning again to it can be like. Testing it, distinguishing it, celebrating it are also in the third step, not the sixth or seventh, because, as nondualism stresses, the direct path seeks to cultivate an awareness of awareness as soon as possible. It is not a far-off, elusive or tricky goal. With a good enough perception of it, much can be reassembled around it.

This turnaround can deepen with a fourth step, which I think of as reframing matters of the soul. The soul level of our experience refers to the complexities that make us feel alive, for good or ill. It is concerned with the ups and downs that knock us about every day. Remarkable advances have been made in charting this interiority, from developmental psychology to psychoanalysis. However, without spiritual intelligence, the very proliferation of this knowledge, and the many associated methods it spawns, can leave people journeying and journaling almost indefinitely. It's good to have a sense of where that ends, which spiritual intelligence supplies.

A fifth step follows because when the soul settles into the being that sustains it, a further development of spiritual intelligence becomes possible. It is also the one that firmly secures the awareness. It involves turning to the tricky, but transformative reality of death, a subject that will be found at the heart of any wisdom tradition of merit. The reason is that mortality reveals itself to be a kind of natality. This comes with the core insight, expressed in the sayings of Jesus quoted above, that clinging to security brings spiritual strangulation, whereas releasing the attempt to hold onto life is the key step to finding it.

Steps six and seven take what has been learned back into the world, as it were, to discover how these truths operate there. Step six argues that spiritual intelligence precipitates a radical shift in our perception of ethics. It must move on from being understood as about morality, defined as doing right, not wrong. That only fosters guilt and shame, and is readily weaponized, and so unwittingly weds us to alienation. The alternative approach, which chimes with spiritual intelligence, is the older tradition of virtue, which focuses on the qualities and characteristics that not only incline us to what's good, but enable us to embrace more and more of life.

Step seven considers how this reorientation of perception might affect a range of matters if it were acknowledged, once more, that we share a boundless spiritual commons. I don't offer a plan, in part because utopias always fail: spiritual intelligence knows the difference between earth shining with heaven and trying to make heaven a place on earth. Instead I describe an attitude or principle that, when cultivated, might spread change from the bottom-up. It focuses on our experience of time and the capacity to befriend crises and irruptions. Spiritual intelligence offers a radically different way of being in the world and, with it, we might come to love realization, instead of being wedded to growth and progress. We might value notions like awakening and conversion, alongside management and development, when thinking about education and ecology.

The seven steps needn't be read in order. If big evolutionary history and the emergence of individuality and freedom draw you, the first two steps will be good places to start. If nothing feels like it has been addressed until the question of death has been faced, then step five could be a way to take the plunge. Then again, if you sense that personal concerns don't touch it without a reckoning of our societal problems, step seven might be a better opener. Alternatively, steps four and six will discuss psychological and ethical concerns explicitly and directly. And if you want to know more about the experience of spiritual intelligence in everyday life, then turn to step three. The steps can be complementary rather than sequential.

The philosopher, Alasdair MacIntyre, is said to have turned the modern approach to ethics upside down when he made this remark in his book, *After Virtue*. "I can only answer the question 'What am I to do?' if I can answer the prior question 'Of what story or stories do I find myself a part?'" So let us begin the steps to spiritual intelligence with a story. It should be of interest. It concerns how we have come to be who we are.

## Step 1

# Telling Our Story

Around a quarter of a million years ago, groups of hominins – the primates most closely related to us today – started to peel away from their evolutionary cousins. In time, they became a new species. They had grown apart from their ancestors and relatives, and felt themselves to be different, which eventually they expressed in the name they gave themselves: Homo sapiens. The first of those words, the genus name, Homo, records the link with the past: Homo sapiens is related to Homo neanderthalensis, Homo heidelbergensis, Homo erectus and others, who, in turn, share common ancestry in primates who lived over 2 million years ago. The second word, the species name, sapiens, catches a departure.

It can be linked to the brain. Although all varieties of Homo had more grey matter than the genus from which they evolved, which is called Australopithecus, anatomically modern humans gathered still larger, globular-shaped quantities of it. Size isn't everything when it comes to mind. Not at all: a not widely known fact is that the brains that flew to the moon and split the atom are smaller than those that thought of creating cave paintings. But sapiens – meaning wise – had a type of brain that facilitated their step onto cognitive terrain previously inaccessible to evolved creatures on earth, and what happened next is remarkable.

Exactly what is much debated. Some say humans evolved language, others an ability to tell stories, others again that a highly flexible imagination began to mark Homo sapiens out. I've concluded that our ancestors became adept at consciously detecting that there is a spiritual commons. They evolved further by growing into an awareness of being that is shared by everything they encountered, because everything they encountered dwells in it, like a myriad knapped flints scattered on the land, each glinting in the light of the one sun.

Back then, this awareness was markedly different from the ways in which people raised in broadly monotheistic cultures would come to know it – although, as we will see, the ways of life preserved by indigenous peoples today are richly suggestive of our ancestors' experience. The crucial point is that Homo sapiens can also be called Homo spiritualis, because an active participation in this implicit dimension of reality was essential to them and us. Spiritual intelligence had become a core part of this hominin's way of life.

That said, and before my story can really get going, there is the question that will already be calling out in a skeptical reader's head. It's the twofold issue that threatens to trip up anyone who tries to say anything general in this area. The first problem arises from the fact that religiosity, as is usually imagined today, is a remarkably recent cultural phenomenon. It can't simply be projected back into the past. The second related problem is that, if religiosity is marked by anything, it is its immense diversity and different forms. What has the human sacrifice of the Aztecs, say, got to do with the Jain who attempts to kill nothing? Or there is the irony that the atheist who tries to debunk religion as if it were one thing, rests their case on a broadly Christian assumption that religion is about one thing that can be debunked.

## The importance of ritual

The way to acknowledge this complexity, and still say something meaningful, has been suggested by scholars such as Robert Bellah and Richard Sosis. It is to look at the deep history of what is now called religion through the lens of ritual. The point about ritual is that it can link the enormous variety of elements that may be part of a spiritual practice – gestures and greetings, devotions and deeds, commitments and creeds. "Ritual is central to religion because learning a religion is a bit like learning to ride a bike," Sosis agreed, when I put the analogy to him. The anthropologist was part of the research group I mentioned in the introduction. "You only really know it when you know it." It's an awareness that is primarily embodied and experienced, and the genius of ritual is that it offers a form of cognition that works from the inside out and, with practice, can lead to all sorts of nuance.

It is the original form of what I am calling spiritual intelligence: the felt conviction that arises from, and gives rise to, a conscious participation in a vitality – or, in earlier times, an ecology of vitalities – that exist within and around the individual. Rituals are such a brilliant way of discovering and developing the presence of such a truth because they are structurally open to truths that are larger than the ritual itself. That is precisely why they are universal, at least in the spiritual domain. You only have to bow towards someone or something instantly to know it. Another sense of life opens up.

Ritual is understood from the inside. It is a subjective form of knowing, not an objective summary of beliefs, which also means that whilst rituals take innumerable forms, and rehearse a plethora of myths that can on the face of it be contradictory, it makes sense to group what they convey together. Religious, or religious-like, rituals in all their variety inform human beings how their life is embedded in a bigger life. In fact, such actions provide a more powerful experience of this intelligence than abstract conceptions can offer. It also explains why contesting propositional truths, as if that were the most important element, is largely a waste of time and, when it leads to bloody conflict, a waste of life too. "Do you believe in God?" "Do you believe in this revelation?" "Do you believe in that book?" People are right when they reject such questions because they do a violence to what they are experiencing.

Bellah concludes that Homo sapiens had realized that the "relentless utilitarianism" of merely surviving "can never be absolute". "The world of daily life is never all there is," he continues in his great book, *Religion in Human Evolution*.[5] Homo sapiens is at least one creature within whom it dawned that the world as it appears is not the world as it actually is. From the rituals, myths, and beliefs that were born, Homo spiritualis was born too. Ritualizing puts the spiritual commons at the center of life, the activity that brought spiritual intelligence. So let's get back to the story.

## *Degrees of freedom*

One way of describing the discovery is to consider a feature of minds called intentionality. The approach is championed by the evolutionary psychologist, Robin Dunbar, who was the lead scientist in the research group investigating human origins that I was able to join. That work forms the basis of my reflections here, though I'm using the insights of others too, to go beyond Dunbar's own conclusions.[6]

Intentionality is the mental ability to focus on something or someone, and it comes with various degrees of conceptual flexibility. A rudimentary form is second-order intentionality, also known as possessing theory of mind. This is the ability to have an awareness of your own state of mind and that of another, hence the "second" in second order. Some animals have it, including apes, as also seems to have been the case for Australopithecus. A sense of what theory of mind enables is indicated by a three-million-year-old collection of fossils known as AL-333. The fossils are the remains of a party of seventeen or so adults and children belonging to the species Australopithecus afarensis. It appears that their group was attacked, possibly by wild cats. The resulting carnage fatally injured some of the company, whom the survivors tended – care that led the uninjured to die too. Their connection with one another was stronger than the threat of death. Theory of mind can do that, as is indicated by comparable reports of the devotion that can be shown by other animals who have it.

Homos first appeared on the Savannah about 2.4 million years ago. They possessed more sophisticated mentalizing abilities compared to Australopithecus, which is to say, they had higher orders of intentionality. By the time Homos such as heidelbergensis and neanderthalensis evolved, less than 1 million years ago, the fossil and tool evidence suggest fourth-order intentionality had become possible. These evolutionary relatives of ours would have been able to hold thoughts a bit like this: "I know (first order) of your belonging (second order) that together (third order) we share with our tribe (fourth order)." The implication is that two individuals would have been consciously able to share their inner life, and that they would probably have been able to talk with some nuance about the life they together enjoyed with others. Different kinds of intelligence were emerging.

You might ask why anyone would want to juggle such a labyrinthine notion connecting I, you, we and others. After all, many animals gain pleasure from their lives together without it. What's the advantage of reflecting on and chatting about the joys and struggles of sociality? In part, verbalizing has value because it nudges up the number of individuals who can sustain social bonds using mentalizing abilities. Again, many animals use other means to form groups, sometimes of vast sizes. Wildebeests assemble in herds numbered by the million and, whilst they make lots of noise, they don't speak. However, primates like us opted for complex inner relationships. In monkeys and great apes, this elaborately experiential approach is fostered by activities such as grooming, though that imposes limits on troop sizes due to the time it takes to comb, pick nits and scratch. Advanced mentalizing is more efficient and, with it, it looks as if heidelbergensis and neanderthalensis could have lived in extended groups of up to about 100 individuals.

In these societies, they made and used tools as earlier hominins like Australopithecus afarensis had been doing for millions of years, though they went further. They decorated themselves with bird feathers and seashells, carefully buried their fellows, and possibly painted on cave walls. Such practices are evidence for the possession of new skills and new states of mind. For example, although many animals deploy tools, from crows hooking grubs with twigs to chimps smashing nuts with stones, Homos developed the ability to make tools like axes and hammers that are much more elegant than is required to fulfil their function. They are a mark not only of aesthetic sensibilities, which naturalists including Charles Darwin have speculated many animals relish when absorbed in the colorful displays of a potential mate, but of the ability deliberately to produce aesthetically pleasing objects. That started to emerge around 500,000 years ago, with the production of what are now called Acheulean tools. Their graceful shaping and pleasing curves are hugely significant. They indicate that heidelbergensis and neanderthalensis had high levels of self-control, that they shared goals and values in addition to instincts and drives, and that they had capacities for future planning going beyond mere habits. They could also hold images of beautiful objects in their minds, which they laboriously manifested in flint and stone. These relics of their lives, inner and outer, are signs of an imagination that does more than inventively solve problems. It desires consciously to bring beauty into the world. They were enjoying more than the relentless utilitarianism of merely surviving.

There is also disputed evidence that Neanderthals knowingly used symbols, which would mark a further development of imaginative power. If they did create shapes such as hand stencils, they were possibly employing patterns and coloring objects with the intention of abstractly evoking the presence of perceptions held primarily internally, in the mind's eye. It would be like the way in which we can use a word such as "mother" or "father" to refer to an individual we know, or a role in a community, or a more archetypal awareness of motherliness and fatherliness that no one person can wholly embody, though they can reflect some of these qualities. That is remarkable. It would indicate that Neanderthals had a sense of vitality that was not only in their minds, or the creatures and places around them, but was in an immaterial world – which is to say, a spiritual world – that the symbols channeled or conveyed. They may have known what Homo sapiens came to know for sure: the world of daily life is never all there is. That said, what appear to be symbols may only be signs, designed to provoke a response, like the yellow stripes of warning on a wasp. We may never know for sure. But given that Neanderthals had a nascent sense of this spiritual commons, that underlines the feature of experience that was to become fundamental to Homo sapiens. Its origins reach back deep into our evolutionary history.

## *Absent others*

The activity of deliberately burying relatives means that we can say with more certainty that Neanderthals had another capacity: to live indefinitely with others who were absent. Death no longer brought active interacting to an end. This is a radical departure in itself. Other animals can remember members of their families, flocks and herds, and often engage in pleasurable and intricate greetings upon being reunited. Elephants will entwine trunks, trumpet and bump into each other. But for a select handful of primates, like Neanderthals, it began to make no difference whether their community was tangible or virtual. "The social life of a chimpanzee takes place in front of its eyes and around its nose and ears," writes Dunbar.[7] "By contrast, for humans it can also take place without any immediate sensory inputs from individuals. Social life takes place in our minds, in our imaginations."

One upshot of this extension of connection over the horizon of what's physically present is that ritual behaviors became increasingly important. All animals have ritual-like habits, and many communicate with one another via ornate displays, but the type of rituals Neanderthals and others practiced would have exploded with internal significance.

In part, that had social effects, which the sociologist Émile Durkheim called effervescence – a sparkling vibrancy conjured by the ceremonies that linger when they end, thereby sustaining and unifying families and tribes.

There was probably lots of time for rituals, as it seems that the business of staying alive took up only so much of the year. There are studies of hunter-gatherers alive today which indicate that about two days in toto a week is spent gathering food, and about another two carrying out practical tasks such as collecting firewood. That leaves three for the ritual and imaginative activities that feed minds blooming and buzzing with their several orders of intentionality. When coupled to the fact that the much-needed effervescence requires regular topping-up to maintain its power to bond, it is reasonable to infer that regular and frequent religious-like activities embedded themselves into these Homo cultures.

Rituals would not have been separated from the rest of life, as if Neanderthals kept an early version of the Sabbath or conducted their rites on a Paleolithic Sunday. The whole of life would have been interpreted through them. "For foragers the food quest is very far from being a matter of efficiently extracting resources from a hostile wilderness," writes Graeme Barker.[8] "They typically operate in an animate, feeling, benign, and articulate nature that is full of 'kinfolk', the plants and animals they seek... The foraging way of life is as much a mode of spirituality as a mode of subsistence."

I've used another contentious word, "culture", and it may

well be that other animals possess limited forms of culture too. What is undoubtedly so is that Neanderthals, and possibly other Homos, would have been preoccupied by the invisible realms that they felt animating the material world around them. The experience of effervescence could be explored in rituals and stories. This would have embedded the sense that the world has an interiority mirrored in their own interiority. The macrocosm around them echoed through the microcosm within them, which is to say they would have had an awareness that the being of the cosmos is the same as their being, that they could test and shape through early forms of myths and rites. "Meaning, imagination, and hope, which constitute our capacity for belief, are as central to the human story as bones, genes, and ecologies," writes Agustín Fuentes, an anthropologist who is championing the crucial role played by conscious awareness in human evolution.[9] Cultures could become as rich as perceptions were deep.

### *Niche discovery*

This flourishing was a response to the discovery of a niche – "niche" being the word that describes the habitat in which a creature lives, coupled to the way it does so. The environmental niche occupied by fish is water and sea, that of birds is commonly the air and sky, and animals with theory of mind can add niches accessed by the imagination. Such an umwelt is infused with multidimensional meanings. Its networks of significance fashion lives very different to, say, social creatures like ants because unlike ants, organization comes with understanding. "All of these enabled our lineage to develop a level of communication-based social learning, a cooperative and collaborative intensity of information transfer that surpassed those of other hominins," continues Fuentes, still with Neanderthals in mind.[10] It embraces novel mental and social resources, like stories and myths, alongside gathered experiences and know-how. Hence, whilst an ant will indicate food sources to its fellows with a dance, a

Neanderthal could share traditions and legends. When coupled to the presence of the dead, the veneration of ancestors would have started being part of everyday life. These communities may have begun saying remarkable things to one another such as, "Our ancestors give us this place."

A dramatic indicator of the implications of this niche comes with the mastery of fire, which no other animal can use in comparable ways. It seems likely that, at first, fire was kept after being sparked by natural events like lightning strikes. Maybe the ancient tradition of ensuring sacred fires stay alight reaches back to this time, possibly 400,000 years ago. Other animals are afraid of fire, so safety is a practical gain that comes with its manipulation, though its value would have risen sharply with the discovery that fire alters the properties of things. Treated in the right way, it will soften meat and harden wood. More remarkably still, fire brings light into the hours of darkness. It is likely that being able to sit around a fire at night introduced a sense that not only objects like flints and skins could be worked, but that the natural world itself might be influenced and manipulated. Fire revealed that the niche Homos had discovered held a power of an entirely different order from spears and axes. Maybe it dawned in their minds that they might contend with the sun, as fire uncoupled the availability of heat and light from the cycle of day and night, counteracting the effects of the setting sun and cold of winter. It smashed previously unsurpassable boundaries. It expanded the spiritual commons. There is good reason to think that Neanderthals used it to take the first mental steps into the less timebound, celestial domains around them – which, as I have defined it, is to say that their spiritual intelligence grew. It is likely that sitting around fires, late into the night, with nothing much to do except discuss and tell stories, they indulged virtuous circles of wondering, inspired by dancing flames.

We are approaching the emergence of Homo sapiens who can

be called spiritualis, though I should first say that most biologists and anthropologists who write about these developments talk about the ability of living creatures to *construct* niches, as opposed to *discover* them. For example, in relation to the use of fire, it would be said its mastery sparked ideas in the minds of our forebears that were projected onto the world around them. So it was not that fire communicated the existence of other dimensions of reality, but that it allowed our evolutionary relatives to fabricate such realms of existence as they shared their fantasies and fictions.

I think that can be challenged as an interpretation stemming from the reductive assumptions of contemporary science read back into the past. Moreover, freer thinkers, such as Erwin Schrödinger, have pointed out that niches cannot be constructed out of nothing. They are, instead, features that appear as a result of an organism's interaction with its environment. Schrödinger wrote about it in, *What is Life?* He proposes that a distinctive feature of living entities, as opposed to inanimate objects, is an ability autonomously to move and exchange matter, energy and information with their surroundings. Animate beings continually interact with the substances and creatures around them, whereas things such as rocks tend to stand still and not change, unless acted upon by external forces. This is to say that much of what living entities do is interact with their niches, which they part discover, and then, part construct. They find and make, preserve and extend them. As Schrödinger puts it: "Life seems to be orderly and lawful behavior of matter, not based exclusively on its tendency to go over from order to disorder, but based partly on existing order that is kept up."[11] Perhaps it takes a physicist to say so because physicists are used to discovering preexisting lawful patterns in nature, unlike biologists, whose starting point is cataloguing the teeming variety of nature that they themselves feel they must organize.

An exception in the latter camp is the evolutionary biologist,

Simon Conway Morris. He sees no reason why the discovery of niches shouldn't apply to the immaterial as well as material world, which is to say to environments of spiritual meaning as well as of malleable matter. Lungs exploit the niche called the atmosphere by discovering it and turning it into a source of energy, and gills do something similar in the niche called the sea. Similarly, the larger brains of Homos can be thought of as resonating with and constructing a niche in the environment we call the mental sphere. What it contains is as real as the material features of the world.

The argument convinces me for a variety of reasons. Take the witness of indigenous peoples, and the Pirahã people of the Brazilian rainforest in particular. When the former missionary and linguist, Daniel L. Everett, travelled to this part of the Amazon, in a bid to make them Christians, he found himself plunged into a niche that his modern mind had forgotten. He arrived in a world of spirits that the people native to it still relate to, in arresting ways. Such subtle beings are fully visible to them, not ghostly or inferred. A tree can simultaneously be a spirit, as can a jaguar. The world seen by the Pirahã has a spiritual concreteness that is as irrefutable to them as, to us, is the value of the colorful paper called money. "I have seen an entire village yelling at a beach on which they claim to see a spirit but where I can see nothing," Everett writes. They live in a niche that is utterly real.

The nature of that reality has been caught on film by the explorer, Bruce Parry. In one scene from his documentary, *Tawai*, he follows a Pirahã group seeking a place to build a shelter for the night. The leader does not scout for a sensible location but instead listens to the spirits of the forest as he walks. "Kaoáíbógí says, 'Do not touch the big trees of the forest,'" he reports to Parry in one moment, Kaoáíbógí being one of the entities that accompany their lives.

If you don't write it off as a collective hallucination, the implication is that Homos became able to interact with a new category of spiritual niches.

## *Meaning-discovery*

Of course, the Pirahã may be confused and partly mistaken about the reality around them, as we will be as well about what we perceive of our surroundings. But I don't think they, or we, can be completely dissociated from it, otherwise no one could survive. So I find a realist interpretation of niches more convincing than the suggestion that they are completely fabricated. We tend not to live in castles in the sky, for all that we can build them, and those who do occupy such fantasies become ill. It does not make sense to say the contents of our minds are simply delusions. You might also point out that there is no evidence that any human being has ever conjured a world out of nothing, be they a creative genius or, for that matter, lost in psychosis. I have worked in psychiatric hospitals. It is a disorientating experience because psychosis wildly and chaotically distorts shared perceptions, not because it is original, which would not be disturbing at all.

Alternatively, and more positively, the realist view accounts for the understanding of poets like William Wordsworth.

> Therefore am I still
> A lover of the meadows and the woods
> And mountains; and of all the mighty world
> Of eye, and ear, – both what they half create,
> And what perceive; well pleased to recognise.

In these remarks, from "Lines Composed a Few Miles above Tintern Abbey", Wordsworth notes that the eye and ear half create what they perceive, though they still perceive reality, which is why the poet can recognize nature as "the anchor of my purest thoughts." Our imaginings may be misguided in all sorts of ways, but they cannot be simply false. If they were, we would quickly become unanchored from reality. As William Blake observed: "Man by his reasoning power can only compare and judge of what he has already perceived." No new perceptions of the world would come into our minds unless they came as perceptions of the world. Human knowledge and awareness would be condemned to turning in on itself in ever decreasing circles. Similarly, the Pirahã leader would threaten, not aid, his people if Kaoáíbógí were just made up.

This is to understand ourselves and our Homo relatives as meaning-making and meaning-seeking creatures, the making being a crucial part of the seeking because it allows us to inhabit the meaning discovered. Fictions develop not only because they aid survival, but because they express felt truths of existence that they also transmit, in circumlocutory, expansively inventive ways. Science does the same today, in the form of abstract theories rather than participative stories, which are put to the test in the laboratory rather than the rainforest.

If you don't accept that these activities of mind are in some way true then you end up asserting contradictions, like Yuval Noah Harari does in his best-selling big history, *Sapiens*. He argues that human gains rose with the ability to tell fictions meant in the pejorative sense, of fanciful illusions, and he defines language as "the ability to transmit information about things that do not exist at all."[12] What he overlooks is that his scientific account of human history would receive the same condemnation if that were so. It too would be a web of useful lies, woven from threads of the deluded communications tool called language, that happens to have the handy byproduct of bonding groups of Homo sapiens who live in a technological age. The medium would fatally corrupt the message, so surely it is better to assume that science illuminates aspects of reality, as rituals and myths do. The fascinating issue is the types of intelligence each offers. As some philosophers have summarized: science asks the abstract question of how, whereas rituals and myths provide a felt perception of what and why. Science generates know-how, rituals and myths know-that – the basis of spiritual intelligence.

## Homo sapiens arrives

To return to our story: the meaning-seeking capacities of Neanderthals, and possibly other species like heidelbergensis, were impressive. However, it seems unlikely that they could have had thoughts, or constructed sentences, such as this: "I think (first order) that you believe (second order) that I imagine (third order) that you (fourth) want me (fifth) to build a fire." Such conceptions require at least fifth-order intentionality and, alongside other abilities, the case for the distinctiveness of Homo sapiens rests upon the emergence of these higher cognitive abilities and the further discoveries that were, once more, to prove revolutionary.

Such a mind enables increasingly complex stories to be told, nuanced rituals to be explored, and – given niches are found and made – subtler aspects of reality to be grasped. The heart of the research being carried out by Dunbar and his colleagues is that whilst earlier Homos had long assembled together to make music and perform rituals, leading to ecstatic states, Homo sapiens continued such traditions and radically upgraded them. This helped our species live in larger groups, of up to 150, the figure now known as Dunbar's number, which brings certain survival advantages. However, it also meant our species could perceive features of reality simply unavailable to earlier minds. Awareness of the spiritual commons took a leap forward, as did spiritual intelligence.

To understand the qualitative differences that become possible with this next set of revelations, consider the parallel unveiling that occurs in childhood development. On the whole, infants gain awareness that other humans have states of mind that differ from theirs in the first five years of life. At first, their abilities can be compared to those of an adult chimp. A child will tell jokes, tease and lie, as activities that are attempts to manipulate another's mind, not just instinctively, but consciously. Simultaneously, the child will migrate from using its name to refer to itself – "Liam juice" or "Olivia comes" – and start using "I" with growing cognitive granularity. "I want" becomes "I think" or "I told". The child's sense of itself deepens and a parent will feel their offspring is becoming more of a person.

This process continues as higher orders of intentionality bring more nuanced ways of understanding. Cognitive growth comes with the consciousness of being dependent, then desires for independence, then capacities of interdependence. Interdependence unfolds into more nuanced capacities again, first with an ability to choose to follow others, then in the struggle to be the author of your own life, and further again to acknowledging that other people have equally valid ways of relating to reality, each with advantages and disadvantages. There is more than one map of meaning, it is realized, much as science and myth can be complementary, not in competition.

With this awareness, the individual is able to shift fluidly from one state of mind to another without feeling they are under threat. Curiosity not certainty becomes their security. Doubt becomes a light, and what might be called a "knowing innocence" is experienced as freedom. The psychologist Robert Kegan has called this level of development, self-transcending.

Such awareness may go further, to reveal that there is a constancy to awareness itself. It is a felt sentience that is both within the individual and shared by others around them. Such spiritual intelligence may lead to the conclusion that there is a universal, conscious container for whatever any one individual is aware of. At this stage, the mind has reached six or seven orders of intentionality and the individual has an immensely subtle sense of themselves, life and others. They will be able to talk about it, though they may also tell you that the best expression of this knowledge is silence – not an empty silence, but one that is full.

Untangling such levels of perception may take a lifetime. It can be advanced by practices that simultaneously develop the self and penetrate life's mysteries. The two go hand in hand, which is why ritual religiosity was the theatre within which our evolutionary cousins and ancestors first stirred the capacity that was to become tremendously refined and reflectively deep.

## *Transcendence*

Consider what it introduces into the experience of group connections. The anthropologist Maurice Bloch has argued that Homo sapiens moved beyond being what he calls a solely transactional species.[13] That way of being in the world can be observed in groups of chimpanzees who sustain long-lasting coalitions and structures of social organization through a nonstop process of exchange, combat and politicking: "I'll scratch my back if you scratch mine" is the popular summary. But early humans went further with the capacity to live as a transcendental species, as Bloch puts it. This is the ability to live in imagined communities shaped by roles that are preserved in rituals and held in the mind. Hence, back-scratching and nit-picking become metaphors.

By way of illustration, Bloch recalls an elder from a Malagasy village whom he knew for a long time. This senior figure became weak and senile towards the end of his life. He stopped being able to recognize people and spent much of his day wrapped in blankets. But he continued to be treated with deference and respect. For example, village rituals did not cease requiring his blessing. His transcendental role lasted long after his transactional significance had ceased. What is striking is that no chimpanzee would continue to bow, literally or metaphorically, to a once dominant individual who had lost in the power play, but the Malagasy elder had become what Durkheim called a "social double": he occupied more than one place in the collective mind.

Homo sapiens routinely deploy this doubling, and it leads to a further unfolding. Individuals, like human elders, can be respected not only because they sanction rituals, but because they carry the presence of gods. A special figure can be regarded as a living superposition of, say, relative, ancestor and deity.

This layering can be observed today. For example, in many African languages, the same word is used for living and dead ancestors; in Indian culture, a husband may be said to be a god to his wife, at least during a puja; and in Christian settings, the name "father" will be used to address a male parent, neighborhood priest, and beloved supreme God.

A community that exists with such an imaginary fosters other developments of inner life. Consider its impact upon feelings of wonder and awe. There is good evidence that monkeys and apes have such experiences. Cameras strapped to the back of macaques in Gibraltar, which can track where the monkeys look, show that, on occasion, they will gaze at sunsets and other absorbing scenes. Interestingly, they may do so even when usually irresistible enticements are nearby, such as fruiting fig trees. The enjoyment of the sunset can overwrite instinctive behavior. In fact, biologists have long speculated that all sorts of animals can be similarly distracted, at least momentarily. In his best-selling book on earthworms, Charles Darwin felt that he sometimes observed the humble creature of the soil pay attention to, and become absorbed by, a leaf mold. Such soils were so attractive that Darwin found he couldn't alarm his worms as usual, with a bright light.

Homos had feelings of wonder and awe. There is no doubt about that, though Homo sapiens had the further desire to investigate its qualities. Cleverer than their forebears at deliberately producing such experiences, they explored the implications of these immersive journeys with a voracious curiosity. You might say that if a dog dreams of the day, and macaques are drawn to a sunset, humans will intentionally investigate what they find beautiful or terrifying, which is to say that their conscious connection with the cosmos intensified. More elaborate rituals and truth-bearing sagas would have been complemented by speaking of, maybe theorizing about, the supernatural, at this stage in our development.

The millennia long fascination with natural splendors such as the life of the sun, cultivated by the mastery of fire, was complemented by otherworldly intrigue, as Homo sapiens came to live not only with their ancestors, but human-animal hybrids, or therianthropes. Creatures such as the minotaur, satyrs and werewolves are their successors. The important detail, in terms of teasing out the development of humans, is that these fantastic beasts are found nowhere in the visible world. Surviving material evidence of them is rare, though when discovered, it is impressive, which is to say such artefacts are still effective: they invite us to contemplate the zone between mundane and spirit worlds. The Lion-man of the Hohlenstein-Stadel is one of the best-known examples, an ivory figure of a supernatural entity that dates to possibly 40,000 years ago. This is about the same time as Homo sapiens decorated cave walls with dancing images of lions and aurochs, which Pablo Picasso remarked have not been surpassed.

Echoes of this joint inner and outer awareness can be witnessed in indigenous hunter-gatherers today. A moment when this distance in time was bridged is brilliantly caught in Werner Herzog's film, *Cave of Forgotten Dreams*. In one scene, an expert in the rock paintings of Australian Aborigines describes travelling with an Aborigine to a remote site, where the expert hoped to document some rare specimens of the art. When they arrived, the Aboriginal man began touching up the images and the expert was shocked. He intervened, fearing the loss of valuable data. What are you doing, he asked? I'm not doing anything, the man replied: it is the Spirit, he stated and quietly continued. His was a consciousness still shaped by a participatory mode of being in which his well-being, the well-being of his ancestors and the spirit world is seamlessly linked. He maintained the images to maintain himself and them.

## Spiritual technologies

There is indirect evidence that reaches back further. Consider the practice of decorating stone tools with ochres. Homo sapiens used these pigments made from iron oxide, as did Neanderthals, though the sophistication of human deployment illuminates a difference. Ochre decoration is the end result of an enormously complex process that is a practical challenge and mental miracle. Making red, yellow and brown dyes is difficult enough. It requires identifying the right types of rock, gathering the oxides that cling to them, and mixing the chemicals with water, or heating them, to produce color. The colors can then be used to change the appearance of a knapped stone, person's body or cave wall, though here is the magical bit: part of the world is, thereby, not only adapted but transformed. Stones, bodies and walls morph and shape-shift. They can become portals to other dimensions. My guess is that if Neanderthals did use ochres to create symbols that evoked presences they physically saw, early humans used ochres to create symbols that channeled presences that exceed the material world. It's the ability that was to make way for what was to become religion and, eventually, science.

The significance of this awareness of more shows up in other ways. Take the activity of storing food and clothing. Evidence from South Africa implies that humans were using ostrich eggs and shells to carry water, pigments and glues from at least 80,000 years ago. They must have used baskets and pottery jars as well, though these objects deteriorate and so aren't found today. Such items are storage technologies, on the one hand and, on the other, evidence of a desire for more than everyday life provides. It could be said that the abundant life of the spirit world led to ideas of excess in the material world. Humans sought to preserve, not just gather; to trade, not just harvest. If this is right, the notion of a surplus was born because of an awareness of spiritual immensity, from which follow further values, such as ownership and property. As Dunbar puts it: "Thinking big is a very human thing to do."[14]

Take a practice such as feasting, which evidence suggests human beings have long enjoyed in sacred places at certain times of the year. They gathered to roast aurochs and pigs, and drink large quantities of beer. To this day, anthropologists have recorded the sumptuousness of these occasions amongst indigenous people. The anthropologist, James Suzman, spent time with the Ju/'hoansi bush people of Namibia, whose feasts include gifts of fish oil, woven blankets, bentwood boxes and copper plates. This is because ritual dining is not only a celebration of means. It is a celebration of awareness and concepts too, made possible because Homo sapiens can appreciate abstractions such as plenty when they see piles of food, and conversely poverty too when they don't – all arising with a developed spiritual intelligence.

This kind of subtlety may explain why earlier Homos, like heidelbergensis and Neanderthals, did not develop their stone and flint technologies once the techniques to make them had been discovered, and were happy to keep making the same unchanged tools for hundreds of thousands of years. They did not have the imagination that sought more of the spiritual commons and so more from their tools. Take heidelbergensis. For 800,000 years, these groups made the same type of hand-axes. They could imagine the need ritually to dispose of them, presumably because flint tools were felt to be sacred. We know this because accumulations of knapped flints are found in clearly designated places, like the site discovered at Boxgrove in southern England. It contains huge quantities of them, alongside animal bones and hominin fossils. But heidelbergensis could not imagine the desire to develop things. They were content in fixed niches.

Homo sapiens was not. Our ancestors had a powerful taste for more, fired by their spiritual intelligence. In fact, one of the byproducts of this appetite, trade, has been offered as a reason Neanderthals became extinct, about 30,000 years ago. If it's right, what happened is that humans simply outgrew and displaced their Neanderthal neighbors. They did so because they had the essentially spiritual concept of a surplus, which led to more food to go round, which led to larger populations of humans. Over time, Neanderthals were squeezed out, unable to imagine the way of life that lay behind the sapiens' expansion and growth. It's even possible that a sort of Neanderthal religiosity contributed to their downfall by keeping them stuck. They may have refused to trade because they saw storage as a kind of sacrilege: the mistreatment of animal and plant beings by stuffing them into clay pots. It might have appeared to them as shocking as the sight of ships supposedly did to indigenous Americans, when the Spanish arrived. They simply did not have the consciousness to understand it, and so demonized the practice, along with the humans who indulged it. Calvin Martin's book, *In the Spirit of the Earth: Rethinking History and Time*, offers an imaginative exploration of this mindset.[15]

## Settling and farming
Not that Homo sapiens is an inherently destructive species. The data suggests that, for much of human history, concepts such as a surplus supported the fair distribution of resources and egalitarian relationships, though it is also right to conclude that, in time, the occasions on which violence was deployed to steal resources changed into organized warfare, which was then used

to subdue enemies and enforce ideologies as well. Only the creature who organizes their life around the spiritual commons can perform such terrible feats. It seems as if this behavior became a regular feature of human culture around 5,000 years ago. It is part of the dark side of spiritual intelligence.

I wonder if a sense of defending the sacred played a key role in the ties that humans developed to particular places, and eventually meant that our ancestors chose to live in settled locations. The thought chimes with the discovery of the ritual complex at Göbekli Tepe and the settlement of Çatalhöyük in Turkey. The meaning of these sites is contested by archaeologists, though it seems clear that sacred structures around which people gathering to feast and perform rites preceded sedentism. This raises the question of why humans wanted to invest so much in certain locations. An acknowledgement of spiritual intelligence offers the thesis that the places became holy because they were sites in which the expansiveness of the cosmos was invoked and reliably known. Human beings could dig down in the quest for meaning, literally and metaphorically. Rootedness is another result of religiosity. Settlements were about securing access to the spiritual commons, as much as anything else.

From that followed the domestication of animals and plants, probably driven by sacred sensibilities too. The role of spiritual intelligence in these developments is worth highlighting because amongst the popular big histories of Homo sapiens written and published today, it has become fashionable to quip that humans did not domesticate wheat and rice, but that wheat and rice domesticated humans. It is suggested that this is an unexpected consequence of what is sometimes called the "oasis theory" of the origins of agriculture, which imagines that humans, plants and animals had to work increasingly closely to thrive in the arid climate at the end of the last Ice Age. The result was that humans became enslaved to securing the well-being of cereals and crops. Harari calls it "history's biggest fraud", arguing that agriculture offered human beings next to nothing in return for the effort of ensuring that a few grasses proliferated across the face of the planet.

What this interpretation conceals is that the evolution of farming was likely an expression of all sorts of distinctly spiritual capacities. It requires the division of labor, another offshoot of the concept of a surplus: I'll do this, and I'll trust you to do that, because together we recognize we're engaged in a sacred process, and together we'll share the proceeds of it. It requires an ability to understand and cooperate with the seasons of the year, to the extent of redesigning the lifecycles of other organisms and making the lengthy commitments required to refashion them. That only comes with a highly developed attunement to the hidden, inner dynamics of nature that can't directly be seen – a capacity akin to detecting the presence of human-animal hybrids. Bringing about lifeforms that otherwise would not exist in the natural world is a god-like undertaking and farming is, therefore, another tangible sign of the distinctive agency arising from the burgeoning spiritual awareness of human beings. It's no doubt why farming is associated with numerous sacred myths, from corn maidens to dying and rising gods. Harari's witty reassignment of agency to plants, as if the crops were in charge, is a good joke, but it conceals more than it purports to reveal and belittles the genius of Homo spiritualis.

The point is that such developments take a specific kind of attention that must be sustained over long periods of time. A ritually or mythological held spiritual vision, felt to be active in the here and now, would have been required to keep proto-farmers to the task for the generations it would have taken for animals and plants to be tamed, and without advanced knowledge of what taming meant, let alone looked like. The practical gains would not be obvious for many lifetimes, which is partly why William Irwin Thompson argued that the development of agriculture was primarily a religious phenomenon, not an economic one.[16] He proposed that links between cattle and the Moon, symbolically revealed in the lunar shape of horns, sustained gradually more intimate spiritual relationships between bovine animals and human beings. Their breeding and slaughter would have been ritualized and overseen by shamans unfolding the inner meaning of monthly and yearly cycles. It is a speculation, and may well be wrong in the details, in particular that it was born of a matriarchal culture, for which there is little or no evidence. But Irwin Thompson was right in spirit and is supported by more recent archaeology. For example, the work of Jacques Cauvin rejects the oasis theory in favor of the emergence of agriculture coming with the birth of new divinities, linked to a change in spiritual intelligence. He proposes that humans came to see themselves as markedly different from the rest of the natural world, though not divided from it, the record of which is the emergence of divinities in human form that are the same age as the agriculture of the Neolithic period.[17] They would signal that Homo sapiens now knew of a realm that was in some way above nature, giving them power and permission, as it were, to change nature. They had stumbled across another aspect of the spiritual commons, represented in deities that had nothing to do with nature, apart from the link with themselves.

As the historian Arnold Toynbee pointed out, to dismiss such possibilities is to be in awe of the technological advances of our era, which can be observed progressing directly year by year. But our ancestors did not know of rapid change. It is also to make the mistake of telling the story of Homo sapiens based upon the evidence of the material artefacts that survive, whilst ignoring the rituals and rites that have become obscured or perished. "Actually, while this mental apparatus is in use, it plays a vastly more important part than any material apparatus can ever play in human lives; yet, because a discarded material apparatus leaves, and discarded psychic apparatus does not leave, a tangible detritus, and because it is the business of the archaeologist to deal with human detritus in the hope of extracting from it a knowledge of human history, the archaeological mind tends to picture Homo sapiens only in his subordinate role of Homo Faber."[18]

## Homo spiritualis is who we are

In this brief history, I have attended to the greater role played not by Homo Faber, the human maker, but by Homo spiritualis. I hope it provides a compelling case for basic links between the evolution of spiritual intelligence, the discovery of spiritual commons, and who we are in our origins. It is an important first step in the reorientation of our lives back to this dimension of existence because it allows us to tell a story in support of its truth and importance.

We have seen how interpreting the past as if it were only about the utilitarian drive to survive misses the ways in which, from the start, Homo sapiens experienced the world as much more than the merely every day. Earlier Homos had entered a mental niche of imagination, where they discovered other worlds that coexist with material reality, and Homo sapiens extended this way of life and spirit. It made us advanced meaning-discovering, as well as essentially meaning-capable, creatures.

The transactional communities of earlier primates became transcendental communities led by elders, ancestors and deities. Our forebears brought dazzling objects of great beauty into the world, which can still take our breath away. Wonder became an experience actively to investigate, not just passively to enjoy. The invisible world of felt awareness, which resonated in the soul as it pulsed across the cosmos, became populated by supernatural beings. They could be approached via magical symbols, which became as important as plain signs, with the seasons and the sun itself not excluded from the magic, following the mastery of fire. In time, the intimate links between spirituality, survival and subsistence morphed into intimate links between spirituality, the sacred and the value of a surplus, which led to the activities of trading and farming. Inventiveness and imagination underpinned everything, as did ritual and spiritual sight. Homo sapiens organized their lives around ritual practices, which brought survival benefits in their wake.

A dark side emerged too, including the organized violence of warfare. That is another aspect of the story of how spiritual awareness became basic to human flourishing. But we have taken the first crucial step in the recovery of spiritual intelligence. It is not a discardable byproduct of evolutionary processes, which nowadays science sees through. It is not the superstitious dross of an earlier phase of human development, which the modern mind can discard like cognitive impurities. It is central. It reaches all the way back across our evolutionary history and only the arrogance that concludes human beings make their reality would conclude it is unnecessary now.

However, there is lots more to say. The way in which we relate to the spiritual commons has evolved further. We must continue the story and turn to step two.

### A quote
"Is man an ape or an angel? Now I am on the side of the angels." Benjamin Disraeli, from a speech in November 1864.

### A question
A variety of big histories are told today, from Adam being created by God on the sixth day of creation, to humankind emerging from a meaningless cosmos as an insignificant species of ape. What big history do you think most directly informs your sense of your humanity?

## Step 2

# Discovering Freedom

A recap. Homo spiritualis, also called sapiens, has emerged. Our forebears have developed an extraordinary capacity to appreciate the richness of the spiritual commons within which everyday life is embedded, and can do so far more extensively than previous Homo species because a newfound intelligence has evolved. It facilitates a mostly ritual-based participation in symbols and sagas that illuminate life shared with ancestors, natural spirits and celestial powers. It has emerged with the discovery and exploration of a niche replete with otherwise hidden vitalities.

Abiding in this domain generates a welter of material possibilities that have also become a firm part of life, from feasting to farming. This religiosity – which takes the form of numerous habits from body paint to sacred greetings – informs, interprets and transmits the animate qualities of the day and night. "It is not about the fine details of theology but is about the raw feelings of experience," Robin Dunbar told me. "This raw-feelings element has a transcendental mystical component."

Another way of putting it would be that whereas nowadays, it is quite natural to assess any claim about an awareness of deities by testing beliefs about them – can you prove they are real, aren't there better explanations, etc.? – in the prehistoric period such a process of thought would have been inconceivable. Instead, we can imagine people experiencing themselves as living alongside spiritual beings that appeared as real as the trees or the sun, and were engaged with in a similarly sophisticated manner as other natural objects – though the phrase "natural objects" would have been utterly alien, too. There would have been no neat distinction between the trees, the sun and spiritual beings since all "things" presented themselves as entities with dynamic, radiating interiorities that, as a porous being too, it was wise to be knowledgeable about. It's a mode of experience in which a shaman donning a ritual mask, say, is not pretending to be a spirit or representing a spirit. They are becoming the spirit. Where we might have thoughts, they had perceptions, which is why Daniel Everett was shocked at witnessing an entire Pirahã village yelling at a spirit, when he saw nothing.

The next chapter in the story begins with a development that will turn out to be fundamental for us today. It makes for a step change in spiritual intelligence that was to become basic because, in time, it fostered a new way of experiencing the spiritual commons, through the sense of being an individual. Indeed, it was this shift that gave rise to the individuality that we now take for granted.

I am going to take some time to consider how that happened, partly because it is fascinating; partly because imagining a different future is greatly aided by realizing there was a different past. Treating it as if it wasn't so different, and that human consciousness has basically been the same across time, is an endemic modern conceit. It comes from physics and is called the principle of uniformitarianism: the assumption that laws of nature have always operated in the same way, everywhere in the universe. As other academic disciplines sought to appear more scientific – or quell their physics envy, depending on how you look at it – they praised themselves for adopting the same assumption. If the object of study were human beings – as is so in the disciplines of history, anthropology and sociology – then human beings would be treated as essentially uniform too, and so wanting what we want now, only suffering from poorer technology and more primitive know-how. This is what produces the idea that myths are bad science, material growth is true growth, and social development follows an upward curve of progress, notwithstanding folds and setbacks along the way.

It leads TV intellectuals to quip that Egyptian pharaohs must have been terrible narcissists because why else would they have built colossal statues of themselves, or that religious founders must have been extraordinarily charismatic fools, because why else might they have been so compelling. They couldn't have possibly been onto something about which I, dear viewer, am completely ignorant, a presenter wouldn't say.

So it is exhilarating to look again, without the prejudice, try to decolonize the past, and see undreamt possibilities emerge. It also creates an opportunity for us to learn about the nature of spiritual intelligence today.

### *All not each*

Take a step back to prehistoric, Paleolithic art, which acts as a record of the earlier human psychology, and consider this detail: it features no human faces. Ancient tribes and communities were clearly fascinated by animals, and when they turned to themselves, they made buttocks and breasts, hands and legs, occasionally hair and noses, but not individually recognizable faces. Cave paintings were clearly not designed to depict identifiable relatives or neighbors. There is no mystery about who the Paleolithic Venus figurines were, as there is Leonardo's Mona Lisa, for all that there is much dispute about what voluptuous female forms were made for. The implication is that no one thought to paint the person called Kushim, to recall the world's oldest name from the city of Uruk. No one had the mentality to do so. Everyone regarded themselves as, first and foremost, a social actor and, in fact, the name Kushim may not have belonged to an individual either but to a role, by which that individual was known. It's a way of doing things that faintly echoes in names today, like Patrick and Patricia. They derive from Patricius, meaning a noble.

The implication is that identity was distributed, and the thesis is supported by the way prehistoric societies appear to have been conspicuously egalitarian – and not because, like modern societies, they aspired to be fair. Rather, these communities were equitable because they did not share the sense that individuals are, primarily, separate or private. Rather, even-handedness was the norm because they were a people – sharing labor and playing the parts allotted to them, with mythic culture sustaining a mutual imaginary of social accord. Rituals meant that no one sought more, as Robert Bellah explains: "The intention would be to celebrate the solidarity of the group, attending to the feelings of all its members, and probably marking the identity of the group as opposed to other groups."[19] The feelings instilled by these customs and activities meant that wealth was pretty evenly distributed.

This is why grave goods of beads and pots, found in burial sites of the time, are all of comparable value: although there are graves for individuals who had particular status, like shamans, there are no monumental pyramids or ship burials, like those that came later.

The places in which people lived are generally alike too. This is so at Çatalhöyük, where the houses are almost wholly uniform, leading investigators to conclude that it was an egalitarian society for most of its history. Only the most recent remains imply that it was on the cusp of becoming more stratified, as if the city was reaching a tipping point, perhaps due to population growth – or to put it from the vantage of spiritual intelligence: the ritually enforced taboos against wealth accumulation were losing their hold on people's minds. But egalitarianism was the norm before this crisis, with people enjoying broad equality not because they lived in a socialist utopia, but because they simply didn't imagine themselves doing anything other than sharing labor, leisure, festivities. There was no imaginative space for individuality to protest otherwise.

Many anthropologists have commented on a similar egalitarianism found amongst indigenous peoples today, which has presumably remained unchanged for tens of thousands of years. Bruce Parry has documented one example, the Penan people of Borneo. They are not strangers to bouts of competition and aggression but, supported by a vivid awareness of the spiritual commons around them, they sustain equitable ways of being that maintain the balance. "And what's even more remarkable, is that this way of structuring society is now widely believed to make up 90 percent of our time on the planet as homo sapiens, thus making it our true, unified cultural heritage," Parry reflects – although, so far as I know, he hasn't factored in the shift in the sense of self to the individuality that is the basis of culture today.[20] As we'll see, once that happens, there is no going back. For a modern person, it would mean giving up the essence of who you think you are.

### Little gods

It's worth stressing, too, that there is no evidence that the level shaping of society was sustained by belief in so-called "big gods", or what is known as false agency hypothesis. I say this because, much like the notion of an enslaving agricultural revolution, it has been common in big histories to propose one of these two mechanisms to account for the emergence of ritual religiosity.

"Big gods" is the idea that our ancestors believed in, and feared, spiritual entities who exercised an overwhelming power to punish human individuals who misbehaved. Such disciplining deities were supposed to have policed behavior in groups and, by threatening massive costs for wrongdoing, from public censure to group expulsion, forced our timid forebears to be good. This is ritual as "a system of human norms and values that is founded on a belief in a superhuman order," writes Yuval Noah Harari in *Sapiens* – and it is mistaken, as Joseph Watts, of the Max Planck Institute for the Science of Human History, has demonstrated. The reason is quite simple: there were no gods big enough to instill such fears until much more recently. "Most societies with big gods have had contact with one of the monotheistic faiths, and that's an idea of God which developed many millennia after the emergence of large complex societies," Watts told me.

The second proposal is false agency hypothesis. It teaches that human beings routinely attribute supernatural agency to inanimate natural things, with the upshot that our ancestors were continually fooled by mounting, erroneous assumptions. For instance, the argument goes, they could have easily become convinced that trees sway due to the presence of dangerous spirits, a conviction that stuck because being scared by swaying is better than ignoring the movement, and one day being pounced on by a leopard. Superstitions were similarly valuable, and so became endemic, the theory continues, because they fed the delusions that supported group bonding: not only must dangerous spirits be avoided but they must be placated by the tribe as a whole. They gave the tribe something to do together. But a passing reflection will expose the silliness of the idea, and that it is contempt for spiritual intelligence that has generated the proposal. Indigenous people, for example, are astonishingly aware of what is going on around them, as is reported by those who have spent time with them. That is why they survive, as we noted in relation to the forest savvy of the Pirahã and the animal awareness of the Kalahari Bushmen. A jumpy hunter-gatherer is a dead hunter-gatherer walking.

### Natural intimacies

The way the porous experience of being human maintained its influence can be detected into the Neolithic period. Consider the contrasting attitudes of the ancient Egyptians and the peoples of Mesopotamia to an innovative piece of technology: the lever. Its impact has been explored by Jeremy Naydler, in his fascinating book, *In The Shadow Of The Machine*.

In Mesopotamia, between the Tigris and Euphrates, levers were used to lift water out of lakes and rivers for a thousand years before they were adopted by those who lived alongside the Nile. The Egyptians knew about the shaduf, as rigid poles hinged across a central pivot were called. The devices enabled heavy weights to be lifted easily and were used away from the river, to move the enormous stones needed for the construction of the pyramids. However, when it came to fetching water from the Nile, the Egyptians resisted them.

The reason seems to have been a dislike of the way the shaduf intervened in the relationship people enjoyed with the god of the Nile's life-giving flow, called Hapi. The shaduf would mean that men and women no longer had to step into the marvelous flood to collect water. The shaduf requires a solitary user to conform to its way of being, by standing on the bank with space to heave it. It undermines the experience of Hapi, which is why it can be assumed people tended not to use them.

There is a distant echo of this resistance when nowadays individuals chose to remove technology from token parts of their lives so as to taste a less isolated, more participative relationship with the natural world. It's a yearning for an older kind of spiritual intelligence. They may decide to undertake an arduous pilgrimage on foot, or swim in wild places not a pool. Some learn to bake bread, so as to knead and know dough. Others will write by hand so as to enjoy the flow of ink on paper and the way it supports their labors. More again will turn to making music, not only listening to it, by joining a choir or learning an instrument. They may never be great musicians but that is not the point, which is to understand more directly the expressive magic of communal melody and harmony. Little wonder there is evidence that practicing a craft improves mental health. The materials communicate their substance. A craftsperson finds it harder to assume they are alone. For ancient people, that would never have been questioned: crafts are not only useful activities but bring people closer to divine aspects of reality, which is why sewing linen or forging iron were intimately associated with gods. Back then, all activities sustained spiritual vision.

In time, the ancient Egyptians did start using the shaduf, and there were gains. The levers became a feature of life in the period known as the New Kingdom. It meant that agriculture became more efficient, and vineyards and fruit trees became more common. Interestingly, the moment that the shaduf was adopted appears to have coincided with the reign of the renegade pharaoh, Akhenaten. He attempted to found a new religion based upon a single deity, the sun disk or Aten. As Jan Assmann has noted, in *The Search for God in Ancient Egypt*, Akhenaten destabilized polytheistic sensibilities, which are generally more commensurate with distributed identities because in the polytheistic pantheon no god stands out, but each plays a part – mirrored by the human community. Akhenaten went against this by emphasizing the unfolding of life exclusively from the potent rays of the living sun. His religious reform did not last, I suspect because people did not experience themselves as individuals who might find a lone identity reflected in the splendid, solitary Aten. They did, though, start to use the shaduf, which suggests that Akhenaten was alert to an embryonic, perceptual shift. His people weren't quite so bothered about their relationship with Hapi.

### *Myths and amorality*

Wariness of electricity is another feature of the ancient world that Naydler unpacks – which brings us to myths as a way of imaginatively entering into the older mindset. Electricity is a form of energy that powers every aspect of modern lives, but it was treated more ambivalently by our ancestors, being both life-giving and dangerous. Thunderbolts and lightning were associated with fire and rain that could equally kindle fire and bless crops, or kill. There were deities who could impart an understanding of these explosive presences, and learning how to relate to them was a central concern of certain ancient mystery rites. The aim of ritually descending into a revered cave, or ascending a holy mountain, was to gain a felt awareness of the relationship between the dark chthonic forces, so as safely to access their replenishing celestial spirit. By observing and sharing in the life of these multifaceted phenomena, an initiate could learn how to interact with them.

This is reflected in the almost universal understanding of the natural world as composed of four or five so-called "elements". Cultures ranging from Egypt to Persia, India to China discussed these phases, aspects or energies, naming them earth, wood, water, metal, air, fire, aether and so on. The details varied and specifics were continually disputed. But the assumption was shared: the cosmos was best understood primarily through the experience of interacting with it, because the driving concern was knowing how to participate in its life, not how best to prod and poke it like as much inanimate stuff. The ancient elements were not types of material but facets of awareness, more qualities than quantities. That is distantly recalled today when someone might be said to have a fiery personality, an earthy humor or a wooden manner.

Ancient attitudes towards the weather are still half-remembered as well. The wind may be described as wild, or the snow as enchanting, and the weather itself is routinely called good or bad, as if it can be for or against us, not merely around us. Interestingly, climate change and environmental fears are prompting a return to the language of beauty and respect when it comes to Gaia's living processes.

There is a further crucial element that Neolithic myths of the seasons highlight. They are amoral. This is another feature of an identity held within the environment, and mediated through the group. Justice, for example, is not about the rights of the individual, but the interactions between all manner of elements within the spiritual cosmos. The human heart of an ancient Egyptian who has died will be weighed in the balance against the ostrich feather of truth and justice, as is shown in illustrations from the famous *Book of the Dead*. But what is being tested is not their personal qualities, as if the balance tipping one way meant they had been a good individual, and tipping the other meant they had been bad. Rather, the heart had ideally to equal exactly the weight of the feather. This indicated that the life of its owner fitted the cosmic harmony, called Maat, and passage to more life is possible. What was being assessed was not whether a person was morally exemplary but the opposite: the aim was *not* to stand out.

The notion of justice as balance is replicated in all sorts of contexts. Ancient Greeks spoke of justice as a form of health, so that if the sickness of injustice infected the body politic, it had to be cleansed of the polluting miasma. In the earlier parts of the Hebrew Bible, the sins of the fathers are said rightly to pass down the generations, which sounds unfair now. Worse still, Yahweh's justice might necessitate acts that utterly offend modern minds as unthinkably immoral. When the people of Israel take the promised land, they are instructed to leave nothing alive that breathes, for example.

Or there is the Code of Hammurabi, the legal text from the First Dynasty of Babylon, in which the king declares: "I installed in this country justice and fairness in order to bring wellbeing to my people." Hammurabi depicts himself as nurturing his people like a creator god, not setting the parameters to which his otherwise independent subjects must adhere, as a modern government must do.

Other civilizations of the same era are similar. To pick just one further example, and acknowledge that this reading is disputed: the oldest parts of the *Analects* of Confucius imply that justice was part of a group ethic, guiding a social rather than psychological notion of self. The leader, Confucius says in

Book 4, goes with what is right because they know that is the way of the cosmos. It is the same mentality that considers filial piety, in which children are devoted to and obey parents, to be a self-evident good.

It's why seeming amorality sets the tone in ancient myths. They are not actually about what is right or wrong, but about how to navigate this and other worlds. Moreover, myths were experienced as being received directly from the regions of existence about which they spoke. They were not imagined but inspired, which is to say breathed or spirited-in by a god, spirit or muse. The process is remembered in the original meaning of enthusiasm, which before becoming an accusation of excessive religious zeal in seventeenth century England, signified the rapt state of inspiration by possession. To speak enthusiastically was to attempt to utter what had first been said by a god. Similarly, no one of this time would have described someone as a genius, but rather as had by a genius – a genius being a guiding spirit.

A glimpse of this difference is offered by a rare survival from prehistory, a poem describing the Sumerian goddess Inanna's descent into the underworld. Her natural habitat is the skies and, for various reasons, she decides to visit her sister, Ereshkigal, who lives under the earth. To do so, Inanna must divest herself of heavenly powers and be exposed in her being to the underworld. That is what it is to go there. In particular, she must subject herself to death. The poem relates how she becomes a corpse, rots like meat, and is hung on the wall by a hook. Then, her wise advisor, Ninshubur, petitions Enki, the god of knowledge and craft. Help is sent in the form of daemons, who look like flies, and they ask for the corpse, much as flies seek dead flesh. They rescue the body and restore Inanna to life. She learns from the experience and sends her lover, Dumuzi, to the underworld for half the year.

Whatever it is about, this is clearly not about individual justice. Poor Dumuzi, for one thing. It is better understood by recalling that ancient people sought ritually to undergo a myth, thereby to discover how together to navigate a path through a world in which life and death, power and impotence, light and lightning coexist. The myth is not an explanation either, as if the ancient Sumerians were trying to describe why there is summer and winter, as proto-scientists. There is ample evidence to suggest that summer and winter were regarded not as predictable changes across the course of the year. They were, rather, living moments that had to be invited, welcomed and secured. Much as the sun's rise and set were the result of divine activity, and could be supported by the sympathetic actions on earth, so the seasons were celebrated as gifts, received with thanksgiving offerings. People abided in life.

Myths that are made for an individual mentality are different. They are typically felt to address one person, perhaps in a heroic struggle for existence. The story of Father Christmas may instill in an unsure child the sense that life can be trusted, more clearly than if a parent were repeatedly to say that is so. The dream of becoming president in a democratic republic can inform individual citizens that their country is on their side, for all that they simultaneously know they never will occupy the presidential palace.

## *Live like a king*

Societies were growing in size. I mentioned that the most recent remains at Çatalhöyük seem to indicate that longstanding egalitarianism was becoming unstable as wealth accumulated and taboos weakened. Studies of ancient peoples whose cultures survive today paint a picture of a comparable transition. What happens is that politics and religion become increasingly integrated in complex, and eventually hierarchical, organizations of society around a central figure: the god-king. It's a first step towards the emergence of individuality as we know it.

A brief sketch of this process, which in actuality is packed with nuance and variation, can be assembled in this way, following the encyclopedic work of Robert Bellah. First, take a horticultural society like the Kalapalo of central Brazil. It has a mixed economy of growing crops and gathering wild plants. The people practice inclusive rituals that sustain the broadly egalitarian shape of their communities. Another relatively flat society is maintained by the Pueblo of North America, whose rituals are mediated by priests, called "religious specialists" in the literature. These figures have a particular function in the community, like shamans, though do not exercise leadership and so aren't part of a hierarchy. The Aborigines of Australia might be said to have found a different but related pattern again, in which the Dreaming offers access to rituals and myths that transmit a level of reality outside of everyday life, thereby bringing stability and meaning directly into everyday life. That directness, as if Aborigines live in more than one world simultaneously, is part of their appeal to modern minds – for all that modern minds are very different.

Signs of shifts from these seeming ancient Edens, in a second stage, can be detected in the Tikopia of Polynesia and the Maori of New Zealand, whose traditions include chiefs overseeing rituals and distributing the surplus after feasting. These leaders enjoy prestige based on the gift-giving, which is not the same as power based on force, though anthropologists note that they are a fixed focus for the common good, which introduces an element of hierarchy into the society. The move from egalitarianism has begun.

A third step is observed in traditional Hawaiian society. Here are found chiefs surrounded by courtiers. It is a specialized type of leadership, suited to organized warfare, which was endemic. The chiefs are respected because of their association with gods as well. The divine realm is mediated by them, and they are felt to belong to a continuous order that reaches between mundane and spirit worlds. In terms of the history of these developments, Hawaii is treated as an example of an early patrimonial state, because these chiefs can become powerful enough to be called a king. A nineteenth century Hawaiian who became a historian of his people, Davida Malo, wrote: "From the most ancient times, religious kings have always been greatly esteemed."[21] Bellah remarks that Malo's testimony is valuable because it offers a rare glimpse of how common people might have regarded this caste of divine royalty. A good ruler, who commanded loyalty, was one who respected the gods, as well as exercised force. They were priest-kings, with power over life and death. They spoke with divine authority, and so can be thought of as men who were gods.

Looking at premodern Hawaiian society is, therefore, to see a transformation underway, Bellah continues. Priest-kings became a remarkably widespread feature across many societies, which became more complex than even the most developed tribal communities of the earlier stages. They became heads of state and, in the largest cases, leaders of civilizations, as seems an accurate description in many places including ancient Egypt, Mesopotamia and Israel, the Aztecs and Mayas, the Inkas and Yorubas, and the longest lasting Chinese dynasty, the Zhou kings who enjoyed the "Mandate of Heaven".

## *The first human sacrifice*

It is a fascinating and, in the details, much challenged period of history and prehistory. One contested question, which is particularly important in the history of religions, concerns the nature of the first human sacrifices, which is to say killings sanctioned by theological imperatives. The historian, René Girard, has argued that individuals who were marked out as scapegoats carried this dubious distinction, the idea being that their symbolic sacrifice could break the cycles of violence that otherwise threatened to consume societies. However, the prevalence of god-kings suggests an alternative theory, that the first human sacrifices were of pretenders to the throne, and their upstart allies. These usurpers challenged the sacred leadership, not only threatening their fellows with violence and chaos, but undermining the ordering of the cosmos, symbolized in the divine monarchy. Such agitators would, therefore, need to be ritually executed, not casually dispatched.

These changes are profound. Where Paleolithic tribes experienced the macrocosm of the cosmos in the microcosm of their lives, Bronze Age societies experienced the life of the cosmos through the presence of the king and state. "It would seem that the shift from tribal to archaic society only became possible when one man focused so much attention on himself that he could claim that he and he alone was not only capable of rule, but capable of maintaining society's relationship to the gods – or, before long – to 'the god'," writes Bellah.[22] "When the Shang king [the Chinese ruler of the second millennium BCE] spoke of himself as 'I, the one man,' he expressed a profound truth about archaic kingship."

This way of structuring society prevailed for hundreds of years, thousands in some cases, and is still remembered in constitutional monarchies today. That said, it is a form of organization that has not, as yet, lasted nearly as long as the egalitarianism that preceded it, to recall Parry's observation that relatively classless tribes and bands existed for 90 percent of our time on the planet as Homo sapiens. And there is a reason for that. Divine monarchs are secretly unstable, a flaw that they try to conceal in pomp. But if the people suffer, which inevitably they do, then a question quickly arises: why can't the king and his god put a stop to it?

The god-king is existentially ambivalent. On the one hand, the focus of power on a symbolic person is revolutionary because it introduces people to an experience of individuality, not known before. They feel it in the exceptional and revered status of the king, and in their newfound status as subjects: they come to know themselves not because of their relationship to multiple gods and sacred places, but through the one human-deity. On the other hand, the potential weakness of these kings, emperors and pharaohs will be apparent and, in times of deep trouble, the dynasty itself may come to be associated with vulnerability and chaos, raising a further question: is the king a proper focus of stability, or is the deity that the king claims to represent the figure to trust? The person on the temporal throne may start to appear as a block to the eternal realm that is above and beyond, underneath and within the transience of turbulent events. Aligning with that dimension of reality becomes the crucial task, at least for those who desire to follow the Axial exemplars, to whom we come now.

## Axial change

The prophets, sages and sannyasins who appear in this moment, about 2,500 years ago, seek to disintermediate the relationship with the spiritual commons, and they do so as individuals. They lambast kings and withdraw from society, treating the priest-ruler as secondary, which is why they are perceived as a social menace. Karl Jaspers, the philosopher who first defined this Axial Age, described it as the period in which human beings "dared to rely on themselves as individuals", which was possible with "man's reaching out beyond himself by growing aware of himself within the whole of being."[23] This spiritual intelligence could detect not only the inner light with which the world of appearances shone, as human beings had known for countless eons, but it could become aware of the transcendence within which the human soul intimately abides; an infinity that exists beyond space and time, though contains space and time. It meant that "hitherto unconsciously accepted ideas, customs and conditions were subjected to examination" so that human beings might be more "open to new and boundless possibilities",

Jaspers continues. They aspired to raise themselves above themselves, in a spiritualized version of the king's attempt to secure the pinnacle of the hierarchy.

Charles Taylor, one of the leading philosophers examining the spiritual meaning of our times, develops the key features of this Axial shift. First, human beings developed a desire to go beyond in some way or other. They may have sought extraordinary experiences, longevity of life, or practices of freedom. Second, they took into themselves the powers that had previously been associated with religious specialists – the shamans and priests – and implied that the spiritual commons is, in principle, accessible to all human beings without them. The boundlessness of spiritual intelligence was relocated from the group to the individual. Third, they recognized that divine goodness is the goal of all people, all creatures and the cosmos itself, even though some spiritual beings, such as Satan or Mara, rebel against it. This contrasts with pre-Axial religiosity, in which spiritual beings tended to be ambivalent or unconcerned about what's good, a disinterest reflected in the amoral quality of older myths. Fourthly, the good as a goal was conceived of in increasingly unitary terms, be that philosophically in terms of being coherent, theologically in terms of being one, or psychologically in terms of being harmonious.[24]

When these four elements are put together, and absorbed into a life, they build awareness of being a distinctive person. The desire to go beyond stresses the value of individuality, as does the equitable access to spiritual insight; the goal of cosmic goodness fosters a desire for henotheism, the worship of one god from the polytheist canon, as well as giving a purpose to life that the individual can make their own. This is often enjoyed in relation to the god to whom a person has a special devotion. Socrates, for example, followed Apollo, not Athena like his fellow Athenians, which was part of what got him into trouble.

Individuality becomes established as a practical way of

fostering spiritual perception, which is not the same as saying that individualism runs riot, as some fear it is doing today. Rather, it becomes possible to choose a way of life that is relatively disconnected from the social matrix. Those who adopt this mode of living seek to dis-embed themselves from society, insofar as that creates space for direct contact with divine life without the mediation of the religious specialists. They withdraw, either actually or internally, so as to connect with the transcendent reality that political and social life can eclipse. Monks, bhikkhunis, sannyasi, devotees, prophets, cynics become a feature of life at the margins. They express a discontent with everyday existence that gives way to emanating an alternative awareness of reality. Their wisdom appeals because it feels simpler, truer and more resilient than the alternatives offered by the god-king or anointed ruler, with the upshot that their teachings revive the spirit of the communities from which the holy figure had originally withdrawn.

Arnold Toynbee has examined how this works. Siddhartha Gautama, the Buddha, renounced the world, sought enlightenment through ascetic practices, before breaking his fasting to discover the light breaking upon him. "And then, after he had attained the light for himself, he spent the rest of his life imparting it to his fellow human beings," Toynbee explains.[25]

Muhammad was born into the Arabian proletariat, from which he withdrew and returned twice, bringing back, first, monotheism, and second, law and order in government. "In the Hijrah [his withdrawal from Mecca to Medina], which has been recognized by Muslims as such a crucial event that it has been adopted as the inaugural date of the Islamic Era, Muhammad left Mecca as a hunted fugitive. After a seven years' absence (AD 622-9) he returned to Mecca, not as an amnestied exile, but a lord and master of half of Arabia."[26]

The Epicureans provide a communal case in point. They emerged in the later stages of the Axial era, during the Hellenistic period, and lived outside of city walls, in communities called the Garden. They knew they were dependent upon the markets and temples of the polis, but they also sought space from the rituals and superstitions, as they viewed them, which shaped city-life. In his letter to Menoeceus, Epicurus is careful to explain that Epicureans are not atheists, in the sense of not believing gods exist, but that Epicureans have realized that the gods are not as people say they are. The people have become mistaken about divine life, Epicurus continues, because social and political life has flooded with false suppositions about what's good and true, leaving citizens unable to grasp the basics. So practice the way of life I advise, Epicurus concludes, in the company of yourself or a friend, "and you will live as a god among men" – which is to say according to divine light and in happiness.

## Myth shifts

Perceptions of the spiritual commons develop as well. For example, older mythic rites are often concerned with prosperity, health, longevity and fertility. In general, there is an understanding of human flourishing that is to do with doing well within natural constraints. The focus is on living in harmony with other beings. The myth of Inanna was to do with death. The benign rule of Hammurabi brought well-being. But the Axial change introduces another sense of human flourishing: the individual can aspire not only to live a good mortal life, but one that integrates immortality. This might mean that the individual befriends death, as opposed to asking the gods to save them from it. It is a form of spiritual intelligence that perceives the infinite and eternal, and as religious thought developed around the new insights, it began to stress how the goal of human life is only fully realized as mortal life passes away, perhaps in an apocalypse, new creation, or escape from the endless cycles of death and rebirth. Even those philosophies that don't focus on other worlds, as are found in Chinese traditions, insist that there exists a version of this world that is perfected by unalloyed goodness. The good ruler and the sage may then be said to have the Mandate of Heaven.

Max Weber called the individuals who adopt an Axial life "virtuosi", and it is a useful expression because it captures how a degree of elitism might be felt amongst the minority adepts. They are in the world but not of the world, to recall the Christian expression. No human individual can completely turn their back on the world and stay alive, though they can put the backs up of those offended by the apparent snub, which is another reason why many of the biographies of Axial figures feature untimely deaths. Pythagoras was mobbed. Socrates was executed. Prophets were stoned. Sages starved.

The meaning of some myths was repurposed to capture this unease. The story of Odysseus' encounter with Polyphemus, the Cyclops, grew in popularity around the Mediterranean at about this time, the mid-part of the first millennium BCE. It must have helped the people by forging an imaginative space within which to adjust to ongoing developments, much as science-fiction tales of renegade robots and dystopian tomorrows do in our times.

The story of Odysseus is well known. He was the wily hero of the Trojan war, remembered for his cunning – his individuality. During the tale, he is trying to return home and Polyphemus got in the way. The monster lives a tough existence, though it is close to the gods, as is symbolized by its one eye, located in the middle of its forehead. At first, Polyphemus has the better of Odysseus, as the representative of older ways of life. The beast imprisons the warrior and his men, though Odysseus makes his escape by twisting a rod of hot olive wood into the one eye, blinding the monster and fleeing.

The story is remembered because the act carries symbolic weight. The warrior signals that his innovative individual deviousness can overpower ancient indigenous know-how, when applied with force. The olive rod is a technology with which he can break free, though at a price: he will feel homeless, as if adrift in the cosmos. Odysseus subsequently spent years wandering the Mediterranean Sea.

Another detail in the story underlines the ambivalence, because Odysseus had told Polyphemus that his name was Outis, or "nobody". When the blinded monster calls out that "Nobody is harming me", nobody takes any notice. It was a good trick, though it is also a curse: Odysseus' wandering becomes entwined with not knowing who he is. The story simultaneously celebrates the new individuality and sounds a note of caution: independence from social embeddedness alienates. Individuality has a dark side too.

Another set of reflections on these changes from the Greek world can be found woven in the work of the great playwrights of the fifth century BCE. Take *Prometheus Bound*, by Aeschylus. It is a tragedy based upon the mythical figure of Prometheus, the Titan who stole fire from the gods to give to human beings so that they could become civilized. The speech Aeschylus gives Prometheus can be read as a condemnation of pre-Axial attitudes towards settlements, the seasons and the skies, and an affirmation of the new attitudes. Prometheus says: "I found human beings witless and gave them the use of their wits and made them masters of their minds... For men at first had eyes but saw to no purpose; they had ears but did not hear. Like the shapes of dreams they dragged through their long lives and handled all things in bewilderment and confusion. They did not know of building houses with bricks to face the sun; they did not know how to work in wood. They lived like swarming ants in holes in the ground, in the sunless caves of the earth. For them there was no secure token by which to tell winter nor the flowering spring nor the summer with its crops; all their doings were without intelligent calculation until I showed them the rising of the stars, and the settings, hard to observe. And further I discovered to them numbering, pre-eminent among subtle devices, and the combining of letters as a means of remembering all things."[27]

## A spiritual democracy

Aeschylus is the first playwright of the Golden Age of Athens, named so, in large part, because of the Axial evolution. Faces in portraiture start to appear at the time, as the abstract, expressionless profiles of human figures found in, say, ancient Egypt, become the individualized, empathic forms of recognizable people. The sculptures of the time offer standards of beauty and representation that still astonish us.

I think the case can be made that democracy was another product of these developments. It may have been a way of trying to ease the inevitable tensions between emergent individuality and traditional society. The usual story, told today, is that democracy was about the state giving power to the people. But, as Greg Anderson argues in his book, *The Realness of Things Past*, it may have really been an attempt to address the question of how new individuals, old clans, a reforming state and the spiritual commons might coexist. The proposed solution was based upon recognizing that all people, in various ways, have a role in maintaining active relations with the gods of the city.

Voting rights were a part of it, though not the most important, which is why no one thought about a universal franchise. Women, for example, exercised their citizenship in the most important and dominant institution within the economy – and the one that obtained until the early modern period, in fact: the household. They were fully involved with its activities, that ranged from producing and trading to educating and arranging marriages. The evidence Anderson gathers supports the conclusion that women knew themselves to be citizens in other ways. They played a crucial role in the rites that sustained the city's connections within the spiritual commons. Women were keepers of spiritual intelligence. "The gods were the ultimate managers of lives and livelihoods in the polis," writes Anderson. Together, they shaped the conditions of existence, controlling the sea and sky, crops and seasonal cycles, marriages and merrymaking, healing and the ongoing vitality of the hearth and home. The modern assumption, that the ancient Athenians were flawed or failed democrats, is therefore mistaken. They did not dream of building the kind of equal society modern nation states have, and judging them in that way conceals more than it reveals. It is another form of mistaken uniformitarianism.

The individuals we now think of as the first philosophers of Greece picked up on the same difficulties of keeping civic life, individual aspirations, and divine dependence in sync. Thinkers like Plato and Aristotle put much of their effort into understanding the implications of new forms of reason and new types of rite that had become important in civic life. They strove to ensure that activities from writing to loving were directed and contained so as not to lose touch with the truths that spiritual intelligence perceives. Philosophy, as opposed to sophistry, aimed to counter abuses. Might was not automatically right, Plato argued. Happiness is found when contemplating the world, not dominating it, Aristotle said.

## *Know yourself!*

There are generally reckoned to have been four civilizations in which the Axial transformation unfolded. They were the originators of the individuality and sense of interior freedom that feel fundamental to us today. Their texts and practices are still enormously powerful when it comes to cultivating spiritual intelligence. In particular, they help us to know what it means at depth to say, I am. We will consider some of how that works now.

The four are ancient Athens, ancient Israel, ancient India and ancient China – although recent scholarship is exploring possible parallel developments in Africa. Take, Orunmila, whom the writer and critic, Minna Salami, describes as the author of the

Yoruba compendium of knowledge known as Ifa. Drawing on the work of the Nigerian philosopher, Sophie Oluwole, Salami observes: "Where Socrates famously said, 'An unexamined life is not worth living,' Orunmila said, 'A proverb is a conceptual tool of analysis.' Where Socrates said, 'The highest truth is that which is eternal and unchangeable,' Orunmila noted, 'Truth is the word that can never be corrupted.' Where Socrates said, 'Only God is wise,' Orunmila too addressed the limits of human knowledge in his statement, 'No knowledgeable person knows the number of sands.'"[28]

The Axial shows up in distinctive ways, but given there are commonalities, they are moments when at least some people began to wrestle with the freedom to say, "I am", as opposed to, "we are". This is why they still inspire. These revolutionary figures could be said to each tackle the challenge, originally engraved above the portico of the Temple of Apollo at Delphi: "Know yourself!" – which takes us to the first Axial civilization on my list, the ancient Greeks.

The famous injunction was presumably originally supposed to dampen any nascent individualism, as a pilgrim walked into the presence of the god. It made you look up and feel small. But when Socrates took it as his motto, he made it into a mantra for liberation: keep asking who you are, doubting your assumptions, and see what hidden possibilities emerge. Plato concluded the practice would lead you out of the cave and to the realization that your life resonated with the unchanging reality of what is good, beautiful and true.

I've written about the impact of the Axial Age in another Axial culture, ancient Israel, in my book, *A Secret History of Christianity*. In short, it led to a complete reappraisal of the old theophany attributed to Moses, who stood before the burning bush that was not consumed and heard Yahweh declare, "I am that I am." It became the founding myth of Jewish monotheism, an awareness of divine reality that became possible to conceive because the Jews of the sixth century BCE began to know themselves as individuals in terms of their relationship to God. That development was, in large part, prompted by the Babylonian exile, which denied them access to the temple of Jerusalem and initiated the dependence upon written texts that led to the writing of the Hebrew scriptures. Reading, as opposed to orality, requires individuality because the one person sits with the texts and wrestles with themselves, as they try to make some meaning of it.

With the formation of Rabbinic Judaism, after the destruction of the Second Temple in 70 CE, the usual way of relating to Yahweh was personalized further. Each individual experienced God's "I AM" insofar as that is reflected within their own sense of self, or "I am". Within Christianity, it was believed that one person had actually lived who completely reflected the divine being, because their humanity was itself complete. That person was Jesus, and the ways in which Christian mystics honed spiritual intelligence will inform us as the story continues.

As will the transformations that sprang from the Indian Axial Age. In particular, the nondualism of Shankara is crucial for the steps we are taking here. Take one of the best known, and earliest, articulations of individual spiritual intelligence as is found in the *Upanishads*. It features a dialogue between the sage, Yajnavalkya, and his wife, Maitreyi – and is the *Brhadaranyaka Upanishad*, 4.5.

Yajnavalkya explains that everything that might be presumed to bring divine or immortal gifts have failed to do so: wealth, love, priesthood, royalty, gods, teachings, rites. None of them deliver. He is rejecting pre-Axial ways. But there is a type of awareness that does, and it requires an inward turn. "It is the self that must be seen, heard, thought of and meditated upon, Maitreyi: when the self has been seen, heard, thought of and meditated upon, all this is known."

Maitreyi is confused. She asks for clarification. What is this turn? Where is this looking? What is this freedom? Why must it be this way? Yajnavalkya speaks directly: "I do not speak to confuse you: this self is imperishable, of a nature that cannot be destroyed... The self is 'not this, not this'. Unseizable, it is not seized; unbound, it does not suffer, does not come to harm."

The divine is located as the most intimate, alert and unfailing aspect of life. It is the knowing that is unbound, not what's known or the knower. This is the heart of post-Axial spiritual intelligence as we know it. Yajnavalkya is inviting Maitreyi to cultivate the awareness of awareness that can be found by the free-moving attention of the newborn individual.

## *The transformation of things*

To develop the insight further, consider how they showed up in the Chinese Axial Age. There were similar developments in the Middle Kingdom, though with a distinctive twist that is illuminating. Differences are helpful, rather than being straightforwardly contradictory, because they can help point towards the core perception.

Heiner Roetz describes the period, again in the middle of the last millennium BCE, as a time in which the people experienced a breakdown of the older order, precipitating a deep crisis for society, the period known as the Warring States. "It shook the traditional worldview based upon the religion of 'Heaven' (tian) and the code of propriety (li) of the Zhou people," Roetz explains.[29] "There is a very clear notion in Zhou texts that something unprecedented has commenced. They speak of a 'chaotic' and 'drowning' world that has lost its foundations and is falling apart. The original 'undividedness' has been 'cut into pieces' (Lao Tzu 28), 'the great primordial virtue is no longer one.' (Chuang Tzu 11)" It was a situation in which, as Chuang Tzu also wittily puts it: "He who steals a belt buckle is put to death, but he who steals a country becomes a feudal lord."

Chuang Tzu is the name given to a Taoist sage and the book

attributed to him. Consider one of its best-known sections, Chuang Tzu's dreamy reflection in which he first wonders if he is a butterfly, and then wonders if he is a butterfly dreaming of being Chuang Tzu. The story conveys the new sense of individual liberty, and the imperative to know yourself, in posing this perplexity: when Chuang Tzu wakes up, he is "solid and unmistakably Chuang Tzu", and yet can't be quite sure of what he experiences. He grows aware of a possible gap between appearances and reality. The reflection insists that there must be some distinction between him and the butterfly, and yet it is hard to articulate what this "Transformation of Things" might be.

Part of the lesson is that relying on oneself requires a toleration of doubt. What is appearance, what is reality? Whatever the answer might be, it is a way that demands an embrace of transitions and transformations, which is explored in another section. Here, a figure called Nieh Ch'ueh asks another, Wang Ni, about how it is possible to know "what is profitable or harmful" without knowing what is right in an absolute sense, which Wang Ni admits he does not know: "The way I see it, the rules of benevolence and righteousness and the paths of right and wrong are all hopelessly snarled and jumbled." It's the Axial anxiety in a nutshell, the fear of the new freedom. But Wang Ni's response opens the Axial possibility.

He says that the "Perfect Man is godlike": an individual who can both embrace the transition of things, as a human person, and stay in touch with an ineffable steadiness that transcends them. It's called knowing the Tao or Way. "Though the great swamps blaze, they cannot burn him; though the great rivers freeze, they cannot chill him; though swift lightning splits the hills and howling gales shake the sea, they cannot frighten him... Even life and death have no effect on him, much less the rules of profit and loss!" He is pointing to a detachment from the apparent and overwhelming immediacy of the present in favor of cultivating a familiarity with a "leap into the boundless".

Spiritual intelligence, as presented and conveyed by Chuang Tzu, sees that the limitless spiritual commons can be a home in the present, here and now, because, in truth, it already is.

Knowing it is likened to a form of active receptivity. It comes with reflecting on the experiences and tasks life brings, in the manner expressed by the concept of wuwei. Another of the well-known stories from Chuang Tzu captures this stance. It concerns Cook Ting. He is a butcher who does not try to solve the problem of how to carve an ox, much as Chuang Tzu does not try to solve the problem of whether he is Chuang Tzu or a butterfly. Cook Ting simply and marvelously dismembers the bull because he follows, rather than insists on, ways of knowing. "What I care about is the Tao, which goes beyond skill," he says. "Perception and understanding have come to a stop and spirit moves where it wants." It takes the inner cultivation of a kind of patient attention: "I size up the difficulties, tell myself to watch out and be careful, keep my effort on what I'm doing, work very slowly..." There's a focus on inwardness and the implicit, which the whole of nature in its mundaneness and magnificence manifests to the eyes that can see it. Therein lies the Axial freedom.

The Taoist path, in common with other Axial innovations, is, therefore, disturbing and challenging. A third passage from Chuang Tzu captures the sense of shock that the teaching provokes, the story about how Chuang Tzu responded when his wife died. His friend Huishi goes to see him and finds him pounding a pot and singing. Huishi is not entirely ignorant of the Way. He argues that it would be enough not to weep over her death, but that singing after her death is going too far. Chuang Tzu explains that he did grieve at first, but then saw that her death is part of the change that is inherent in her birth. That sight of change, even in the extreme moment of his beloved wife's death, led to a transcendent perception: "Now she's going to lie down peacefully in a vast room." The response is a powerful and provocative sign of the practical depth of immersion in the Way, a path that an Axial individual can choose to pursue. The choice means not just living by the Way, which the myriad of things does anyway, if – in the case of humans – typically with resistance. A path is open so as to live by the Way with conscious participation and transcendent, steady awareness.

Chuang Tzu contrasts his liberty with Confucian ideas. He characterizes them as a blind focus on "external things" and ritual. He wants his readers to move on and is fully aware that many of them follow Confucianism. So he argues, with typical provocation, that it's utterly inappropriate to try to ameliorate or manage the challenges of the age because that only leads to unexpected, and probably damaging, consequences. "You can't bear to watch the sufferings of [this] age, and so you go and make trouble for ten thousand ages to come! Are you just naturally a boor? Or don't you have the sense to understand the situation? You take pride in practicing charity and making people happy – the shame of it will follow you all your days! These are the actions, the 'progress' of mediocre men... But what good are these actions of yours? They end in nothing but a boast!"

Chuang Tzu is different. He can sing of the Way because he participates in it afresh, with a deliberate wuwei, and so he becomes an adept of spiritual intelligence and established awareness. "It exists beyond the highest point, and yet you cannot call it lofty; it exists beneath the limit of the six directions, and yet you cannot call it deep. It was born before Heaven and earth, and yet you cannot say it has been there for long; it is earlier than the earliest time, and yet you cannot call it old." He can accept the sufferings of the age because he knows of more. "Your life has a limit, but knowledge has none."

## Coming to today

We have travelled a long way in time, chronologically and

psychologically. We launched the trip with Alasdair MacIntyre's question about the need for the story, or stories, of which we are part, and we have identified two: the evolution of Homo sapiens as always, already Homo spiritualis, and the emergence of human individuals who understand themselves to be receptive and alert to the transcendence that is their origin and goal. It is the felt presence of every instant, when attuned to.

The spiritual commons in which our Paleolithic and Neolithic ancestors embedded a shared way of life, can be known now as opening within each truly liberated individual. Indeed, the conscious opening of the spiritual commons is the finding of the type of freedom that is the opportunity to align with truth and goodness.

But what of our predicament today? Jaspers observes that, "It is impossible for man to lose transcendence, without ceasing to be man."[30] It is a stark, alarming warning. Ignorance about what spiritual intelligence sees as the reality of the spiritual commons might be said to be the defining feature of our times.

Jaspers makes his remark because he lived in the period in which that loss is apparent. He lived in our age – which brings us to our third step, and recalls MacIntyre's second question. Once a backstory is clear, MacIntyre asked: what am I to do? How might the source of the self, and the timeless liberty articulated by Axial figures and others since, be known afresh? How indeed?

### A quote

"Freedom and slavery are mental states." Mahatma Gandhi, *Non-Violence in Peace & War*.

### A practice

Nowadays, freedom is talked about in several ways. Some say it is about choice, to opt for this or that way of life. Others about expression, to say whatever seems right. But can you turn inward and find another type: the place of freedom within you that is always free to long for what's good and always free to turn towards it?

## Step 3

# Seeing Reality Is Simple

The inner life of a waking day simmers with myriad moments colored by attention and distraction, cleverness and foolishness, thought and vacancy, despair and delight. Emotions and notions shift and switch from one to another almost as frequently as a secondhand ticks. The frothy amalgam of states of mind includes what's valuable, unimportant and destructive. It gets us out of bed and into a spat online. Though what spiritual intelligence notices is that the busyness is pervaded by an atmosphere of being.

It is a steady everywhere from which the myriad thoughts and feelings spring. It's a field around the particles flitting in and out of existence. It's a carrier wave for the modulating signal. It's a well of meaning from which words and speech are drawn. When that infinite source is identified and befriended, something else is found within it too: freedom.

This freedom is not of choice or expression but recognition. It grows as spiritual intelligence becomes established. Further, it transforms the hubbub of the waking day's flux, making it seem like variations on themes in an infinite piece of music. The rhythm, timbre, counterpoint and instrumentation constantly change. At times, the harmonies stretch to breaking point as a bit of it collapses into dissonance. But remarkably, even then, for the person to whom that has happened, a brief reflection can be enough to reconnect with the wellspring. "Ah, I became lost, distracted, absorbed!" A step back. "I am the experiencer, not the experiencing." To know that is to touch freedom.

This is the significance of free will. It is not a fantasy of unlimited choice. It is not an escape from what has shaped you, be that your genes, your upbringing or the stars. Rather, it is the ability to craft such constraints into fresh manifestations of being, much as a painter works with a few basic colors to create inventively delightful scenes. And it's available every second of the simmering day. If you tend to be hard-hearted, try softening. If you feel closed off, reach out. If you habitually go left, turn right. And always keep an eye on the atmosphere of being. It's the one constant in the who of who we are.

The passing preoccupations and pressing problems may even come to be loved as the weave within which this space is found. In truth, the two aspects of consciousness – the appearances and its essence – can be distinguished without the need to divide them, much as a sequence of numbers and the set of those numbers is the same.

The difficulty is when the details fog the wider reality, making being alive an arduous journey ruined by the anxiety of travel. That condition can set in for years, during which someone may never be conscious that they are thinking, feeling, anticipating, remembering. But the possibility of stepping back, knowing yourself and seeing the spiritual commons reflected in the mirror of the mind, never ceases because the present moment, as opposed to the past or the future, is the only moment to take stock, and it is always here, now. Nothing changes in the past, because it is past. Nothing changes in the future either, because the future is a dream projected from the present. But if you can attend to what's happening in this instant, and focus on the fluidity of its dynamics, then options for alternatives, springing from awareness, present themselves.

So if for a while, you forget it, recall it. It is unaffected by your absence. To imagine anything can be done to harm it is to be like a child who panics when their ball rolls under a chair, thinking the toy has been snatched or vanished. Being cannot cease to be, any more than something can come from nothing. It is the biggest of big projects. It is boundless.

### *Chocolate waves*

I walk to the corner shop. It's taken me all morning to write that. I want some chocolate, and become engrossed in a petty debate with myself about whether to buy one bar or two. One would be a nod to restraint. Two would be more honest because if I buy one, I'll only be back later in the day for a second. "But," my pulsing mind continues, "a second walk would be another stretch of the legs, away from the screen, and another moment in the sun to bathe in its living light." "Pah!" comes the next beat. "You say you value nature's outdoors. Pull a few weeds from amongst the daffodils or gather last autumn's leaves. They've had six months to brown and dry."

Then I chuckle and remember. The bouncing waves across the ocean of awareness. Momentarily, I leave my thoughts to their tussle, and sink below the surface to flow down into a wider rings of being, recalling Rumi's image.

I detect the rest and calmness that never ends. I appreciate that it is not a reality I can hold in my mind, because it holds my mind in it. It's not mine or yours, it's more than me and you. I enjoy the reunion and am grateful for its patience: I've already returned a dozen times that day and could have done a dozen times more, if I'd remembered. Not that being cares whether I consciously return once, a thousand times, or never.

That is another tremendous thing. The aspect of life of which spiritual intelligence is aware cannot be pursued, as the positive psychologists tell us we must pursue happiness, or economists growth, or religious folk salvation. It can only be discovered. That is infinitely better because it means the cosmos is fundamentally a place of abundance, not transience, resistance or scarcity.

The truth is close to what John Stuart Mill intuited when he remarked that the ability to do without happiness is a smart way to realize the pleasure of happiness, for the reason that joy comes with living, and flees when made a goal in itself. Then again, he was wrong to conclude that experiences of happiness are helped by stoically embracing fate or, conversely, admirably doing good for others. That was probably a result of his godfather and father, whose fanatical utilitarianism was fixated on results and consequences. They drove John Stuart into a period of suicidal depression in his late teens, he explains in his *Autobiography*, from which he was saved by something utterly different: the poetry of William Wordsworth. The verses were a revelation. They spoke to him of the delights he had failed to notice in his drive to succeed, and which are not a product of success but are just there for the taking. He spotted the beauty of nature and, with that, "states of feeling... the very culture of the feelings, which I was in quest of."[31]

Mill was sensing the presence of the domain in which feelings dwell: the very culture of the feelings is the soil from which seedlings of sensation sprout. He was alert to the very culture, not the feelings, as what he must strive to know. That's the spiritual commons. That said, he couldn't quite drop the need to quest. As he entered his twenties, he dreamt of improving the physical and social conditions of humankind so as to spread the beneficence he had discovered. That is worth doing, but not because it will bring cheer. Endemic sadness and mania in the developed economies he envisaged, in which we now live, demonstrate that much. What he had missed was that Wordsworth was nudging towards spiritual intelligence's more radical perception, "Of something far more deeply interfused". It is that which "impels All thinking things, all objects of all thought, And rolls through all things."[32] There is a dimension of reality that is drawing us back to itself, and that is the one thing above all others worth knowing.

The ancient Greek Stoics knew it too. They did not make the mistake of thinking that what is now called stoicism could be forced, as if the best way to approach life is to grin and bear it. They taught that emotions can be tolerated when they are known as eddies in a strong current of goodness, which they named the Logos. It was their word for the spiritual commons. They realized that goodness would have its way, which can sound deterministic, until you realize that it is goodness having its way and that there is no other way to go. Actively go with the flow, they advised. Trust it, rest in and work from it. Therein lies freedom.

## *Experiences of unity*

I'm on the way to the shop. My thoughts about Mill and Wordsworth swell and break. The waves don't cease, though at least I can feel something of the tremendous energy within them.

A moment later, another bit of turbulence forms. It's different. I'm at the traffic lights now, and someone is standing next to me. I stop alongside and what comes up is a kind of test. If the being that is most fundamentally me is the being that is most fundamentally everything, then can I detect the same being gently radiating from this person too? I won't look at them. That would be weird, and they are unlikely to be actually glowing. But can I discern the shared ground as a shared presence?

It's not a mad question. I have felt shots of it before, most vividly in relation to a tree, a deer and the sun. The tree moment came in the sort of formal setting you might expect such breakthroughs to happen. I was sitting in the meditation room of The Buddhist Society in London during a scheduled period of silence. It was windy and warm outside, and I could hear the trees rustling. The sound became indistinct as I sat, morphing into white noise, and in a moment of reverie, which is not what I was supposed to be having as the intention of such sessions is to practice watching thoughts rise and fall, the world suddenly flipped. I was the tree. Though that's not quite right because any distinctive I-ness went. It's more like the tree and I were a bigger I.

Afterwards, I thought about Dante's experience in paradise,

which he describes in the *Divine Comedy*. He is surprised to discover that the souls he encounters in the brightness of heaven know the longings and joys of those around them as keenly as they know their own. Further, he realizes that they do so not because they have a capacity for direct telepathic communication, like as many well-wired nodes in a network. Rather, they are alert to the inner life of their fellows because they are, first, alert to the awareness that fills the heavens. Reflective consciousness pervades this realm like air fills a room or light fills the sky. It is the understanding out of which paradise is made, and to sense this bubbling insight around and about is to be in heaven. One ramification of the experience is that when Dante hears souls singing, which in heaven they do with the slightest prompting, he cannot tell whether they say, "I" or "we", "my" or "our". He hears the singular and plural pronouns simultaneously. The souls have not merged, though they are not separate either. This state of connection is the means of their telepathy, and my guess is that I had a fleeting, faint experience of that linking with the tree.

On another occasion, a similar spin of awareness occurred with a deer. I was walking through a woods, again lost in thought, and remember suddenly coming to a halt. It was as if I saw myself from a tree up ahead, standing to my waist in bracken. A moment later, the I in the bracken looked up and, now back in myself, I saw a deer standing by the tree from which I had been looking. Its eyes were locked onto me. Another second and it bounded off. I was sad because I would have loved a further second to appreciate the communion.

A third experience, with the sun, was more sustained. Again I was walking, which is an activity I like because it combines action and inaction: doing something physically helps me worry less about what I am doing mentally. I was looping a small south London park and as I came around a corner, the sun appeared over the tops of the houses. I was dazzled visually and jolted psychologically. And then there was the about turn. I knew that its being there, and my being here, were part of the same being, which is everywhere. Its blaze was not just sunlight. Its light was the gleam of being itself, joined with the luminosity within me.

In the interests of transparency, I must confess that at the time I had been reading a lot of William Blake. I was grappling with what he meant by not seeing the sun like a golden guinea levitating in the sky, but as a glorious company of the heavenly host crying, "Holy! Holy! Holy!"

I'd concluded that what Blake didn't mean was that he was having a peak experience because he had long known how to access the imagination, not just flights of fancy. This is imagination as the way we see the world. The scientific imagination is one form of it, within which everything becomes an object to measure and study. The artistic imagination is another. In Blake's case, the spiritual imagination perceives everything as an image within which can be discerned entities including angels, world souls, the spirit of the times, individual souls, deities. This is what it is to have cleansed the doors of perception, as he famously remarked. He could always see the sun as the heavenly host. His mind could intentionally shift to that observation, such was his spiritual acuity. My identifying that the sun's sparkle shone in me, as it rose above the rooftops, gave me a better sense of what Blake was onto. I might have come to that awareness without him, though I was much better prepared and open to the possibility because of him.

It is also the case that the park I was looping is only a mile or so from the trees in which he saw angels, though I don't think that proximity had much to do with it. Eternity's sunrise is not bound by place and time, though I suppose certain times and places can make us more porous to perceptions of it.

How Blake could see in this way is further illuminated by William James' discussion of conversion. His fascinating book, *The Varieties of Religious Experience*, notes that people switch their imaginative lenses continually, which is why the world seems so different across the course of a week or day. You only have to consider your mood at home, at work, or upon waking at four in the morning, to spot how it alters. The same life, your life, can appear calm, tedious or terrifying in each of these zones, which is why some people try to stay in one and avoid others, by becoming a workaholic, say.

That variety is normal, if distressing, James explains. But conversion is another matter, and it is this which William Blake understood so clearly. Unlike the daily shifts, it is a permanent alteration in worldview that, in time, reforms the whole of life as its influence percolates across every aspect of a person's inner life.

James theorized it in this way. He proposed that a conversion reorientates the individual around a center of forgotten energy. I'm calling that the spiritual commons. Whilst this quality of being remains unrecognized, the individual forms their habits of perception and experience in relation to other ideas, which seem more present and right. The scientist has beliefs about empirical testing and, because they are convinced this methodology is the royal road to truth, they apply it to as many parts of life as possible. When you have a hammer, everything looks like a nail.

That certainty can, though, be usurped by the forgotten energy. When what was marginal takes center stage, it ignites, prompting a period of reorientating uncertainty and struggle. And if that uncertainty and struggle leads to the mind dropping to a new equilibrium, because it has discovered a more stable state of being, conversion occurs. It is called a conversion when it proves permanent, or at least becomes permanently accessible to recall.

A common example is falling in love which, with its ecstatic feelings of unity, is related to the oneness known by spiritual intelligence. The world never looks the same after the first crush, regardless of whether it lasts. The experience wakes the individual to another way of being in the world that seems possible to return to. Similarly, Blake's awareness of the sunrise was not the whimsy of a fanciful mind, any more than love is a foolish exception to the norm of human depravity. It's a realization, and hugely valuable.

## *Peak experiences*

So, I am at the traffic lights. There is someone standing next to me. Can I feel them radiating being? I am weighing up the odds. Who knows? I might be on the verge of a blast of enlightenment, such as was described by the monk and spiritual writer, Thomas Merton. That would be a boon on an otherwise average day.

Merton tells of one day standing in the shopping district of Louisville, Kentucky, on the corner of Fourth and Walnut, when this happened: "I was suddenly overwhelmed with the realization that I loved all these people, that they were mine and I theirs, that we could not be alien to one another even though we were total strangers. It was like waking from a dream of separateness."

The moment made him want to laugh out loud. It filled him with immense joy. "And if only everybody could realize this! But it cannot be explained," he writes in *Conjectures of a Guilty Bystander*. "There is no way of telling people that they are walking around shining like the sun."

That's true. Only a conversion, or flip, or flash of spiritual intelligence can tell them that. However, if I were to see the person standing next to me, right now, shining like the sun, and maybe one or two others walking on the pavement, that would be nice.

Then, I check myself. I am feeding the desire for a peak experience and that is high risk. As Mihály Csíkszentmihályi remarks in his seminal study of the states he called flow: the enjoyable quality of such episodes, and the flood of meaning they bring, is addictive. The minute there's a craving to return to that zone is the minute the individual has become captive to a version of reality, which is therefore the minute they are on the verge of rejecting reality itself. At best, that person has turned from life, for a time. At worse, they are coaching themselves to become unable to cope with the ambiguities of existence, when the spiritual sun appears not to shine. All they want is the lovely flow state or peak experience to reappear, one more time. And then one more time, and another. The excitable manner in which the discovery of the steady awareness of spiritual intelligence is often discussed, as a moment of stunning enlightenment gifted to the few, similarly does most people a massive disservice if it makes them want one too. It can be like that, on occasion, and sometimes with stunning effects. Joan of Arc said she was united with infinite life and felt herself to be its agent or hand. It provided her with the energy that carried her on the extraordinary transformation from her peasant class to leading the armies of France. But such blasts in history are the exception that prove the rule.

Blake's humdrum ecstasy, which was not really a stepping out of himself, as the word ecstatic implies, but a stepping back into that within which everything unfailingly abides, is more useful. It can see a world in a grain of sand, and heaven in a wild flower, to recall Blake's summary from his *Auguries of Innocence*. Julian of Norwich explained the same in relation to a hazelnut. She saw a ball of about that size lying in the palm of her hand, prompting her to contemplate it "with my mind's eye" and ask: "What can this be?" The eye of her understanding received the answer: "It is all that is made."[33]

The exceptional status often given to enlightenment may be a result of something – a lingering effect of the Axial Age, when knowing yourself and finding the immortal was felt to be an option only for committed renunciates or highbrow philosophers. That might have been true two thousand years ago and more, because ancient people needed to achieve something that is a given for us now: individuality. They had to wrestle with an egalitarian mass consciousness, that was wary of rebels and policed by taboos which condemned those who did not fit in with the whole. Socrates had a good word for what he needed in conformist Athens: a place that is "atopos", or nowhere. In the speech that he made to his fellow citizens, when they put him on trial, he said that his inner voice, or daemon, had told him to withdraw from public life, and it was right to do so. He needed to find himself aside from the hive mind. The jury, unsurprisingly, was not impressed. He was explicitly challenging its crowd mentality. They ordered the hemlock. But today, we are at a different point in the history of human consciousness, in part because of the atopological pioneering of Socrates, Chuang Tzu and others. Our difficulty is not withdrawing from others, which the modern mind does spontaneously, but connecting with that which is more than both. Participating with the inside of the world, not closeted in our own interiorities, is today for the many, not the few.

That suggests another reason that enlightenment can be talked of in misleading, if understandably, euphoric tones. It is not that waking up transports the individual elsewhere, but that it transforms what is immanent and nearby. And it can happen in an instant. Hildegard of Bingen tells us that she saw "the heavens opened" in this way. She spoke of suddenly seeing the life of all creatures, and perceiving the way in which everything is related and connected. And this makes a real difference. She knew human beings to be "living sparks". She produced symbols and images that convey archetypes for the divine. She could hear music, and compose it, as a reflection of paradise.

The discovery that this is possible appears revolutionary, as if it would turn the world upside down, but really it is to realize what the world is like when understood the right way up. I think that it is for this reason that the contrast between a sense of unity that is ecstatic, and one that is seemingly humdrum, with a preference for the latter, is insisted upon in developed wisdom traditions. A pictorial representation is shown in the ten oxherding pictures of the Zen tradition. The crucial detail is that the first and the last pictures are the same: the seeker is on their own. In the middle eight images, they seek the bull, which stands for the agitated heart and mind, so as to understand it, and thereby transcend it, though that enables the individual to return to everyday life, not leave it. As Buddhist teacher Martine Batchelor explains: in the first picture, the oxherder assumed spirituality was found in a particular somewhere, whereas in the last they realize that spirituality is everywhere.[34]

The biography of Teresa of Ávila charts a parallel discovery. In her early life, she experienced union with the divine ecstatically in brief bursts, during which she was slain. The famous sculpture by Bernini, which shows her moaning in ecstasy whilst being pierced by an angel's spear, captures the state that she eschewed as she grew older. The deepest dwelling of union, which she describes in her mature book, *The Interior Castle*, is earthed and embodied. She knows it whilst with the pots and pans of everyday life.

Did you ever really believe that your everyday thoughts were exclusively your own, and never thought by another? Did you believe the philosopher who argued that there is no way of telling whether the color you call "red" is the same redness seen by others? Did you ever fear that you might be the only person on the planet who is not a robot, and teeter on the edge of a solipsistic void? That is enlightenment's big reveal. Creation has not fallen into a lost state, as believers in a transcendent, distant God often say, because human beings haven't become uncoupled from life, though they do forget they are part of it. And that doesn't change how being embraces all. It can tolerate what is sinful, evil or proud. As Ibn 'Arabi explained: if you actively walk away from God, you are only discovering how vast the presence is. To believe people could become separate from the origin of life is really a confession of not trusting the omnipotent and omnipresent origin of life.

That said, right now, at the crossing, I don't particularly feel the being that shines in me shining in the person next to me. And anyway, the traffic lights have turned red. I silently wish him well, thank his guardian angel for not minding the intrusive speculation that we might momentarily comingle, and cross the street. And, in a flash, another set of thoughts grab me.

## Suffering and selfhood

Why is there this sense of separation? Need there be alienation? Doesn't it produce pointless suffering? For sure, it causes the background suffering that most people feel from time to time, and some feel most of the time, but not so as ultimately to be pointless. Rather, it is the painful stage through which individuality is born, the consciousness of separation that is able freely and consciously to step back into participation with being itself. To rewrite John Stuart Mill: it is not happiness that is a byproduct of life, but suffering. It is the almost unavoidable consequence of the evolution of the metacognitive awareness of awareness that comes with the higher degrees of intentionality, first experienced by Homo sapiens.

Our forebears spoke about it in myths. Take the story of Adam and Eve eating of the fruit from the forbidden tree in Eden. They did so because the tree was there, much as a mountaineer wants to climb Everest. As Yahweh would have known as well as any parent, putting the tree off limits was tantamount to fixing a label to it: "Desire!" Adam and Eve are archetypal human beings because they follow the urge that characterizes Homo spiritualis as a whole. We are the creature who wants to peer over not only near horizons, but the most distant ones. The further away, the better. Or as someone once remarked: we are the creature for whom our own existence is too small for us. We want all of existence. That's what makes us different. That's the ambivalent benefit of having spiritual intelligence. It can fulfil and lead astray.

The Genesis story can be interpreted as telling of the way that consuming the fruit revealed the niche in which we live, and how it is marked by three related capacities: self-awareness, separation and self-transcendence. Hence, according to the story, Adam and Eve eat the fruit and immediately make loincloths from fig leaves. Their first impulse, after the shock of awakening, is to hide. In particular, they do so from Yahweh, the divine presence, who is walking through the garden at the time of the evening breeze. Their self-awareness provokes, at first, shame and suffering. They have become individuals in a way they weren't before, but at the cost of a rupture.

That last bit, about Yahweh walking through the garden on the evening breeze, is a lovely detail and speaks to the depth of the alienation. The word in Hebrew for "breeze" is also the word for "spirit" and "breath", which is to say that Adam and Eve no longer spontaneously recognized the inner presence of the breeze as the spirit or breath of God and the cosmos.

Their inquisitiveness leads to their loss of the Edenic state. However, what they have found is also the means by which communion can be recovered. As Yahweh continues, in the second section of the myth that is usually forgotten: human beings have become divine by eating the fruit, insofar as self-awareness brings not only suffering, but also consciousness of immortality. There is gain in self-awareness as much as separation, symbolized in the reference to a second tree in Eden, called the tree of life. The freedom that led to eating the fruit and stepping away from being is, at the same time, the freedom that enables stepping back, boosted with new knowledge about the nature of being.

Comparable tales that reflect how individuality is based upon a rupture can be found in other traditions. Plato tells the tale of Atlantis, a city that is destroyed by the gods because its citizens were overreaching themselves and threatening the harmony of Europe and Asia. The *Upanishads* record tensions between traditionalists, who advocated duty based upon caste, and renunciates, who abandoned status altogether.

Modern philosophers have described it in existential terms. Kierkegaard called relating to oneself as oneself the "sickness of despair", though added that it brings "the infinite erectness or loftiness of spirit." Schopenhauer argued that the fundamental being of reality, which he called the will, needs secondary representations of reality "to become conscious of itself, just as light becomes visible only through the bodies that reflect it."[35]

Chuang Tzu makes similar observations. The Taoist philosopher speaks of the memory that all things, at their origin "in ancient times", were good. Competitive living tends to take humanity away from this unity, which is why, when he is offered work in a palace, a haven for intrigue, he retorts that he would prefer to live in mud. In the dirt he is free to continue the cultivation of the personal qualities that resonate with the original goodness, that is, with the Tao. It can be known inwardly by the restored individual, when it then reveals itself as the interiority of the cosmos, unalloyed. This is a conscious rediscovery of the primordial undividedness, which is an advance, because the spiritual commons can now be known by an individual, not just shared by the collective.

That is so because, in ancient times, people acted and lived within the Tao without awareness of it, Chuang Tzu explains. It meant that qualities of intention and self-consciousness were absent. "The True Man of ancient times did not rebel against want, did not grow proud in plenty, and did not plan his affairs. A man like this could commit an error and not regret it, could meet with success and not make it show. A man like this could climb the high places and not be frightened, could enter the water and not get wet, could enter the fire and not be burned.

His knowledge was able to climb all the way up to the Tao like this," Chuang Tzu continues. The sage is describing a state of relative innocence, which I think is akin to the egalitarian unity of pre-Axial consciousness.

This explains why he adds further details which suggest the people of ancient times experienced life very differently. It was as if they didn't have minds to repel the Tao. "The True Man of ancient times slept without dreaming and woke without care; he ate without savoring and his breath came from deep inside... The True Man of ancient times knew nothing about loving life, knew nothing about hating death." It sounds remarkably like the contentment explorers report finding in indigenous peoples, and see eroded as they are exposed to the so-called "outside world".

There was no conflict between aboriginal humanity and the Tao – "man and Heaven did not defeat each other" – though that contrast with now means the myth can speak of the experience of deliberately returning back to the Tao. It must be found intentionally, and that means not by virtue of birth, but freely. Chuang Tzu's way is to dare to be an individual in the richest possible sense, neither being individualistic, nor relying on customs and conventions, but fully rejoicing by abiding in the way of heaven once more. That is the gift of spiritual intelligence as it can come to be known.

### Simplicity and soup

I've reached the corner shop. I am not consciously participating in the Tao, mostly because by the glass doorway is a stack of tins bound in cellophane wrapping. The shopkeeper has been to the wholesaler and my gaze skates across the pile. Yellow and green cans. Sweetcorn. Beige packaging. Chickpeas. And then my eye is caught by red with a hint of orange. Tins of tomato soup. I love tomato soup. The waves in my mind proudly crest because I know something about tomato soup: it's food made of a philosophy.

I learnt this from a Michelin star chef who was discussing how to make soups. He is of the minimalist school of cuisine and said that if you want to make a mushroom soup you need two ingredients: mushrooms and cream. Likewise, if you want to make tomato soup, you need tomatoes and cream. The recipe is simple, he continued, because soups have a secret: the reduction.

This is a simmer during which the essential ingredients are heated just shy of a boil. The broth slowly thickens as water departs, intensifying the flavors. It is an ancient technique. Roman cookbooks described wine, grape and vinegar reductions. They form a basis for all sorts of sauces and potages, which is to say that reductions are akin to essences. They simplify to yield more. A good reduction grows in depth, richness and tastiness, and the same can be said of the process called refining, which comes from the root "to make fine". Oil, sugar, salt, iron are purified to reveal their core finery.

Tomato soup amuses me because it is a reduction in almost the opposite sense of the way the word is most commonly used today, in which to reduce is to strip away to the bare bones. It's a thinning, not thickening, of reality.

Take reductionism in the scientific domain. It eliminates and granulates, often to the point at which the original object of study is lost. A reductionist studying consciousness will assert that consciousness can be explained by understanding how nerve cells fire, without worrying that no nerve cell ever felt or realized a thing, which is the heart of consciousness. Alternatively, a physicist might say that the cosmos gives up its secrets as its building blocks are smashed by being spun in a particle accelerator.

This is the paradox of scientific reductionism. Parts are only comprehended in relation to the whole, but much science is focused on tearing them apart. It does lead to discoveries that are often fascinating. But it should never be forgotten that the behavior of bosons will tell you nothing about the behavior of baboons, let alone the intricacies of their primate consciousness.

There are further insights about the nature of spiritual intelligence hiding in the refinement of tomato soup. Its reduction could be linked to the origins of the word, which is not to fragment, but restore or lead back. It is the meaning used by the alchemist who sought the philosopher's stone that could transmute base metal into gold. It was generally reckoned that this required purity of heart on the part of the practitioner, as well as the correct chemical know-how, which in a way doubles us back, and links this richer sense of reduction to another key word that is often misunderstood: simplicity. This is the simplicity, or purity of sight, that penetrates the confusion of appearances and distils what's basic.

The simple soul has this capacity, explained Marguerite Porete in *The Mirror of Simple Souls*. They are not naïve. Rather they have a penetrating clear-sightedness which, in the spiritual case, means such a soul "swims in the sea of joy: that is, in the sea of delight, the stream of divine influence." They have spiritual intelligence. Similarly, theologians insist that God is the simplest entity of all, which is why God can be behind and within the full splendor of reality's variety, intricacy and vitality. God's is the opposite type of simplicity to a stone, say, that doesn't do much beyond keeping still, because divine simplicity does everything and, if you are a theist, everything depends upon this complete openness. It is like the rich simplicity known by my minimalist, Michelin starred chef, only instead of it being a simplicity of taste, it is the simplicity of ubiquitous, fecund presence.

In truth, fruitful simplicity plays a key part in scientific discovery. Picture Isaac Newton sitting under the apple tree. He realized that the force which causes the fruit to fall is the same as the force that causes the moon to orbit. The law of gravity was born of this simplification of appearances, which could be perceived by his penetrating mind, though it was an account of two phenomena that looked very different on the face of it. The eighteenth century philosopher, Anthony Ashley Cooper, drew the only sensible conclusion from the link: underneath it all, nature herself must be elegant, simple and beautiful, as is the human mind, which can detect nature's simplicity because it is shaped by a comparable simplicity. "Harmony is harmony by nature," Ashley Cooper wrote, which is a bit like observing that only awareness is aware, consciousness is conscious, and insight is insightful. It is an insight from spiritual intelligence.

So, in truth, spiritual intelligence is what enables scientists to give conscious expression to the intelligence of the natural world, summarized in theories like laws of nature. When it is understood in this way, it yields a type of science that is about relating to nature, rather than controlling it. A spiritually minded scientist is a person who has the vocation to surface the knowledge that nature conceals in its "endless forms most beautiful", to recall Charles Darwin's phrase. The aim is to "give up to us the most intimate secrets of life," as Henri Bergson put it in *Creative Evolution*.[36] This is what science does, at its best, Bergson continued. Science's secret is that it loves nature for nature's sake, not because of the ways in which nature can be exploited.

To say so might seem obvious. But there are scientists arguing it needs to be positively, explicitly affirmed because of the way science is going. They are thinking particularly about the way computers and AIs are deployed. To get at their concern, consider the way in which the supercomputer DeepMind was recently heralded with making a great breakthrough. I'm not thinking of winning games this time, but the achievement of making remarkably accurate predictions of the shapes formed by folding cellular proteins. The result was described as a "gargantuan leap" in the leading science journal, *Nature*, partly because the advance will aid bioengineering, partly because protein structures have almost wholly resisted prediction before. But it's worth asking what kind of leap this achievement of DeepMind represents? In particular, the AI didn't produce any insights into the nature of protein folding. Its calculations were enabled by the extraordinary computer power at its disposal, not because of a simple, penetrating perception. This might not appear to matter, until it is recognized that the power of DeepMind to predict nature comes at the price of not appreciating nature. It delivers predictive power at the cost of cognitive distance.

The mathematician and former president of the Royal Society, Michael Atiyah, called this exchange a Faustian pact. "The devil says: I will give you this powerful machine, it will answer any question you like. All you need to do is give me your soul" – by which Atiyah meant the faculty by which human consciousness can understand nature because it resonates with nature. Of course, no scientist would say they are selling their soul, or would want to. "Nevertheless," Atiyah continued, "the danger to our soul is there, because when you pass over into algebraic calculation, essentially you stop thinking; you stop thinking geometrically [by which he meant in relation to simplicity, elegance and beauty], you stop thinking about the meaning."[37]

If this path of brute calculation is pursued, it seems that the better AIs model nature, the stranger nature will become to us. Indeed, some scientists already make a virtue out of the incomprehensible conclusions of science, almost implying that the weirder the truer. We might be living in a cosmic simulation. We might be holograms. These proposals are new forms of alienation and must be related to the fear that the impenetrable workings of nature, and computers, are soon to turn against us, in an environmental or technological apocalypse. This future is a nightmarish projection of the present, and may be a self-fulfilling prophecy if it narrows the imagination and erases other ways of living.

I fear it every time I hear someone say life is becoming more and more complicated. My fear is that this is an expression of anxious disconnection, rather than a true observation about the way things are going. People in distress in the therapist's room say something similar. "I can't cope!" The panic about complexity rises with a loss of the ground that holds together the riotous multiplicity of things within its underlying, simple unity. And wisdom traditions testify to it: connection. They speak of "the great ocean of truth", to recall Albert Einstein's phrase. Like the reflective mirror of a telescope, spiritual intelligence can gather the rays of light that radiate from the fact of existence and bring them to a focus, so as to make intuitive sense of them.

Arnold Toynbee reckoned that when disconnection becomes endemic, civilizations decline. Cultures and societies stagnate as their people lose confidence that their intellectual grasp, aesthetic insights and practical achievements are in tune with reality. In place of the spiritual dynamism from which the civilization first sprang emerges an existential fear that the world has become an enemy. Strident, popular voices will preach that there is no spiritual commons. Civilizations then focus their energies on merely perpetuating and extending themselves, which becomes unsustainable. Collapse follows sooner or later, and recovery only comes with a renewed vision of reality. It takes not only new insights but new types of insight, which are actually old types, made new.

This is why the Axial figures are associated with collapsing civilizations, to which they brought fresh vitality and flourishing. Socrates was born into an Athenian empire that had over-reached itself; the Buddha and Mahavira lived during a time of disintegrating Indic civilization; Taoism and Confucianism coalesced with the Warring States period; the Hebrew prophets drew their fire from the crisis in Judah; and Muhammad refashioned devotion and government in Arabia. It is easy to conclude that today we live in another period of technologically extravagant but unclear, purposeless extension, which is why

Alasdair MacIntyre has concluded that the Western world awaits a new Saint Benedict, recalling the father of monasticism who seeded purpose after the collapse of the Roman Empire. What needs to be rediscovered, Toynbee said, is how to connect via the means of simple sight and felt unity. To know that you are part of a place, not an alienated visitor, makes a huge difference because an immersive relationship liberates energies that bring new visions and transmutations of the soul.

## Reality's open system

Tomato soup can keep my mind occupied for a long time. Then, I recall that I came to buy chocolate. I walk into the shop.

The sweet counter is to the left, past the cash till, and also past a cluster of religious objects that the owners keep to accompany them through the day and night. One stands out to me. It is gold, I imagine made of plastic, and is decorated with a few studs, also presumably plastic, resembling dull diamonds. Its centerpiece is Arabic calligraphy. I read, "Allah."

I know no Arabic by sight, apart from this one word. I love to spot its w-shaped sweeps and final confident stroke, and it reminds me of the basic statement of faith in Islam: "There is no God but Allah." The simplicity strikes me as preserving the essential mystery of God that spiritual intelligence loves. The negative way of putting it, "there is no God but...", is illuminating.

Spiritual intelligence is often associated with these negative traditions, or the apophatic, as it is called. This is because it discerns what lies within the everyday, though also dwells beyond and beneath the humdrum. It speaks of what falls outside of words, though is the reason words convey meaning. It's why abstract expressions like "being" and "existence" are never far from the exploration of the spiritual commons, though they are really failures of expression – tolerated only insofar as the felt presence they aim to evoke is implicitly understood.

It's a bit like the Zen master who points at the moon, and reprimands the Zen student, who has become preoccupied with the manner of the pointing. They have forgotten to follow the direction of travel towards what is being pointed out.

Plato described the difficulty well with his analogy of the divided line. It is a straight stroke divided into four parts of increasing size. The first two, smallest segments represent all that can be seen in the visible world – the first representing shadows and reflections; the second, animals and plants. The second group of animals and plants are more real than the first of shadows and reflections, in the sense that animals and plants have life in them, rather than being echoes or doubles of life, as shadows and reflections are.

The second two segments of the divided line, the larger ones, represent objects that are not subject to decay and change, and so in this sense are more real again. The third segment holds thoughts like numbers and shapes, and the fourth holds understanding, like knowing what is good and true.

Another way of putting it is that the first smaller segments represent things that can be guessed at ("what's that shadow?") or deduced ("it's tomato soup"), and the second larger segments represent things that are settled ("a triangle has three sides") or basic ("the divine simplicity"). In this fourth section lies the spiritual commons.

The paradox which the divided line shows is that what is good, true or simple is both hardest to pin down, at least in abstract terms – try defining what is good or true; we've had a go at simple – though it is also the case that you know these qualities immediately you see, feel or benefit from them. They feel elusive until you feel them directly. Then you know that nothing is more real. They are in the biggest section of the line because they are closest to being itself. They are not subject to coming and going, but rather always have more to give.

Reality is an open system. Dante glimpses it in the *Divine*

*Comedy*. He ascends through the heavens and sees a pinpoint of infinite brightness from which all light radiates and shines. It is reality's never depleted origin. Arjuna is close to overwhelmed by the same perception when, in the *Bhagavad Gita*, Krishna says: "You will not be able to see me with your natural eye, so I give you a divine eye."

The philosopher, Ludwig Wittgenstein, captured the perception: "We feel that even if all possible scientific questions be answered, the problems of life have still not been touched at all. Of course there is then no question left, and just this is the answer. The solution of the problem of life is seen in the vanishing of the problem." He is often taken to mean that the answer to the riddle of life is that there is no answer, or that turning life into a question is the problem. But I think he is pointing to a subtler truth: the issue is how you are looking, and where. If you look to being itself, rather than the questions, the problem of life vanishes, for that is to see life itself.

It is why silence is associated with spiritual intelligence, the silence precipitated not by saying nothing but having too much to say. "Those who know do not speak. Those who speak do not know," avers the *Tao Te Ching*. "Not how the world is the mystical, but that it is," Wittgenstein continued.

Plato called it the third thing, often cited as the tertium quid, "third" because it is implicit, and so easily overlooked or forgotten, though it is the invisible presence that supports everything that is manifest. A lover and the beloved draw on the loving. The knower and what's known depend upon knowing. Moreover the lover and the beloved, as well as the knower and what's known, are not separate from loving and knowing, but are directly experiencing loving and knowing. They are dwelling in being, for all that they forget. Such is its grace. Incidentally, this threefold sight is the reason the Christian tradition calls God the Trinity.

Our intelligence is a reflection of a greater intelligence,

much as the creatures who thrive in a rainforest or kelp forest live in accordance with the intelligence of the surrounding ecology. It calls us and much of the joy of knowing comes with the experience of being joined with that expansiveness. It's why Archimedes leapt from his bath when he grasped the displacement of water and cried, "Eureka!"

This understanding doesn't take place in the mind, let alone the brain, though the mind can come up with useful words and images, on occasion. The key point is that there is something upon which reality depends. It is unconditioned, over which we have no power, which is why contact with it offers peace.

The chess grandmaster, Jonathan Rowson, catches a lovely experience of this inner beauty in his book, *The Moves That Matter*. He writes: "Outer beauty experienced through the senses and inner beauty experienced through the heart, mind and soul are different things. They do intersect, for instance when we feel awestruck by nature, but we find it much easier to talk about what *looks* beautiful than what is beautiful. I am often asked for instance about my favorite chess sets, but rarely about my favorite chess moves. I would much rather play a beautiful move on an ugly chess set than an ugly move on a beautiful set. In the first case, the action would feel closer to the truth."[38]

If you can feel why the beautiful move is closer to the truth, you can see what Plato was driving at. Aristotle summarized it well, when he said that the greatest, universal truths are hard to grasp because they are simple, though when they are seen, it is like eyes adjusting to the brightness of a summer's day. Suddenly, everything is seen with an unanticipated clarity.

There is a difference to detect between artificial and spiritual intelligence in this. If artificial intelligence is mostly about solving problems by spotting patterns, and emotional intelligence is mostly about relating to feelings by understanding them as opposed to being swept along by them, spiritual intelligence turns to the steady presence that runs through, above and under it all. This awareness is transformative not because it is successful at what it does, like an AI; or because it fosters flourishing, like emotional intelligence, though it might. Spiritual intelligence enables the individual and groups of individuals to become increasingly aligned with the deeper pulses of reality. It takes us to the shoreline of knowledge where learning becomes a type of listening, consideration a type of resonance, and personal change a type of expansion. With spiritual intelligence, education becomes an activity that seeks to draw out and recollect, rather than pour in and test. The disposition of the individual towards themselves and others matters more than their ability to handle propositions, which is why spiritual intelligence is discerned in someone because of the quality of what they radiate, rather than the cleverness of what they say. It is available to all.

Conversely, overlooking or denigrating spiritual intelligence is disastrous. Without a lively sense of it, people and whole societies can self-organize around skills rather than values, success instead of purpose, talents more than calling, pleasure as opposed to delight, fending off rather than letting in, what's transient instead of what's timeless, what seems empty as opposed to full, what must be earned rather than what is copiously given. Bucket lists become the measure of a life rather than convictions, miscellanies are preferred to deep dives, if soulful and imaginative wealth is felt to be illusory or unreliable. It's the worldview that has been driven by the kind of science that explains everything in terms of survival and reproduction, because it has forgotten that survival is valued only because existence already shines, and reproduction is desirable only because it's a chance for more individuals to love the infinite.

### *Power or participation*

The current preference for power over participative perception reaches back to the late medieval philosopher, William of

Ockham. That's strange because he was also a Franciscan friar, greatly influenced by his spiritual hero's sympathy with nature. Saint Francis could see the sun as his brother and the moon as his sister. He could praise wind and water. He could perceive spirit in it all. But the humble friar's living love of the world became the medieval philosopher's austere observations of it. Francis' simplicity, which was an ability to see the beauty in everything, became a universal acid, designed to dissolve whatever appears extraneous and unnecessary, particularly the esoteric, spiritual vitalities from which Francis drew so much. The loss is caught in the violent metaphor by which William of Ockham is remembered. Ockham's Razor shreds entities not detected directly via external appearances. The inner life of the cosmos, its dancing soul, which so delighted Francis, is a victim of this ruthless, epistemological pruning.

The aftereffects were dramatic. The word subjective used to mean "existing in itself", which is to say drawing directly from the ground of being. Francis could sing to the sun as brother and the moon as sister because, like Blake, he recognized his shared life with them. Alternatively, it captures how nature was thought to be an artform, with a capacity to give form to matter from within itself, much as a human artist forms matter from without. Thomas Aquinas expressed it by comparing nature to a self-assembling ship: "It is as if a shipbuilder were able to give to timbers that by which they would move themselves to take the form of a ship."[39] This is nature's subjective power. It means that nature can be known from the inside out, as much as the outside in, and to be as full of spirit and meaning as the inner life of a person. Conversely, to describe something as objective used to mean it is merely an object, and so unreliable and empty. The older sense hangs around phrases like "to be treated like an object". But then, following Ockham and others, the two words swapped meaning. In modern usage, subjective came to imply idiosyncrasy and bias, and so doubtful, and objective came to mean impartial and cool, and so true.

It's another indicator of the disaster that follows loss of the spiritual commons. The reversal in the meaning of subjective and objective has done immense damage to human beings, partly because it doesn't stop there. Doing away with the inner life of the cosmos is a step towards doing away with the inner life of people. Individuals still have inner lives, of course, but they come to prefer to talk of dopamine rushes rather than feelings, as if the objective description carries more validity than the subjective. They will turn to brain scans before Sappho or Rumi when asking about love. They will ignore activities that have great value, like a walk in the park or saying thank you, until a scientific study confirms the value. Much suffering, ennui and purposelessness has been precipitated by not trusting subjective experience, and so failing to be conversant with it, discerning it, being curious about it.

Reversing the meaning of subjective and objective is also a philosophical mistake, because so-called objective truths are the ones that keep changing. The history of science is the story of their continual modification. It's what makes science interesting, and is why scientists continually announce that they are on the edge of another great discovery. And they may be. But to find something that is unchanging and reliable, you have to rediscover subjective experience. Of course, I am not thinking of the ups and downs of inner life that are also there – its idiosyncrasies and fears, its simmering flux. But rather the constant awareness and steady presence that is the background and underpinning of consciousness; the atmosphere of being. You have it. I have it. All humans have it, even when asleep, which is why an alarm clock wakes us. As the potter and philosopher Rupert Spira summarizes: "Any honest model of reality must start with awareness. To start anywhere else is to build a model on the shifting sands of belief."

Allowing yourself to return to an awareness of being,

prompted by a sunset, a vista or tins of tomato soup, feels like drinking an elixir. It is if it enables a return to an everlasting source of life, because that's what it does.

I've completed my journey to the shop to buy chocolate. I had left the house, crossed at the traffic lights, paused as I spotted the yellow, green, beige and red-orange cans, walked pass the cash till with its religious trinkets, and reached the sweet counter at last. And now here, what happens? I change my mind.

Such is the simmering hubbub of waking life. I had wasted my time debating whether to buy one bar or two as I walked down the street. I should have known that a myriad of thoughts and feelings would intrude over that five minutes. So what did I actually buy? Anything? I did. Not chocolate, but that philosophical reduction, that reminder of simplicity, that manifestation of the source of life: a tin of tomato soup. It's time for step four.

### A quote

"Know yourself or Know your being, because you are not you but you do not know it." Awhad al-din Balyani, *Know Yourself*.

### A question

A common piece of advice is, "be yourself, be natural!" There is a true impulse behind the injunction, though being yourself assumes, first, that you know yourself. Have the reflections in this chapter questioned or deepened who you take yourself and others to be?

## Step 4

# Settling The Soul

The film, *Inside Out*, is one in a series of brilliant movies about inner life from the Pixar studio. It features a girl named Riley who, at the age of 11, has to move from Minnesota to San Francisco because her father has a new job. It is a near disastrous experience for her.

Life to that point had been close to perfect, which in terms of the story means that her inner life is dominated by good feelings. The genius of the film comes in the way that is depicted. It shows her basic emotions anthropomorphized as Joy, Sadness, Fear, Disgust and Anger, with Joy in charge, at first. Joy has the upper hand because Riley has core memories of love and connection, which are in turn the building blocks of her personality.

These character-emotions are a virtuosic representation of what Carl Jung called complexes, defined as part personalities that are active in the regions of ourselves of which we are less conscious. These emotionally toned fragments tend to be mono-dimensional and have a semi-autonomous life of their own, and so can often appear to come and go as they please. They major on warmth, reactivity or longing, and form because, as children, we are vulnerable to experiences and so tend to absorb and introject what happens to us without much processing or filtering. A pleasant or affirming experience or environment, such as the loving gaze of a parent, builds into a complex that interprets life positively. A painful or traumatic incident or period, such as the loss of a parent's affection, builds into a complex that interprets life warily. It is a way of modelling why the early years are so important. It shows how moods can vary across the course of a day. When a good complex is front of mind, the sun shines. When a bad one takes control, clouds form.

These feelings tend to be the aspect of the soul of which we are most directly aware, and when they are the only aspect of the soul of which someone is aware, the tendency is to assume that they are all that the psyche contains.

By soul, I mean that take on ourselves that nowadays is predominantly experienced as interior and felt: the quality of being alive and knowing you're alive, with fears, connections, movement, hope. This is not soul in contrast to body, as if the soul were an immortal fragment that floats off when the body dies, though it is often talked about it in that way. In truth, it's a shorthand and misleading because soul is the feature of being human that we know as the individual, personal presence of ourselves or another. Soul can also be noticed when looking at physical objects that are striking, or enjoying music, or in the moment an insight is understood, also called an "aha" moment. Our embodiment is one tangible expression, the physical manifestation of a person's psyche, which is why it reveals itself as, say, laughter lines on a face or the bright eyes of someone who is inwardly free. William Blake caught it when he observed that there is "an immense world of delight", which is closed or framed by the five senses of embodied perception. The empirical world is not separate from soul, as if dualistically split off because of being matter not mind. Instead, it presents soulfulness to us in experiences of sight, sound, smell, taste and touch. "Man has no Body distinct from his Soul; for that call'd Body is a portion of Soul discerned by the five Senses," Blake writes in *The Marriage of Heaven and Hell*. Similarly, Wittgenstein remarked that our attitude towards other human beings is of them being a soul, not having a soul, of which their body is a picture. Soul is the immediate dynamic within experience, thoughts, wisdom. It is not an object that's located anywhere specific, but is the specific subjectivity of a living thing that emanates from them. Spiritual intelligence perceives that soul is different from the presence of being itself, but that's a point to which we'll return. For now, something is about to go very wrong for Riley.

### Breakdown and trauma

She sets off for San Francisco wrapped in the comfort of her apparently perfect family: her mother and father reinforce her soul's sense that the world is, basically, there for her and can be trusted. But then things start to unravel. Their new house is dilapidated, unfriendly and contains shocking sights like dead mice. The family's removal van is delayed, which means Riley can't surround herself with familiar objects that might comfort her. Worse still, the pizza takeaway, which might have offered her a treat, puts broccoli on all its pizzas. It's a good joke, though speaks to Riley about how life is starting to feel poisoned.

At first, her inner complex called Joy manages to keep the happy show on the road. Being a mono-dimensional part personality, Joy has only one script, which contains an endless store of tips for happiness, derived from pop psychology. "Treat each day as a gift!" Joy pipes up, along with, "Find the fun!" When Riley wanders into her drab new empty, attic bedroom, Joy intones: "An empty room is an opportunity!"

But Joy wrestles with secret anxiety, which is what happens when happiness is the extent of your mood repertoire. In the interactions between Riley's inner characters, it shows up as Joy repeatedly worrying that Sadness is about to touch one of Riley's memories and turn it from golden to blue. Interestingly, and in one of the subtle touches that make Pixar movies so great, Sadness is always following Joy around, like a shadow. When Joy notices Sadness crying, Joy can't tolerate the tears and so misses Sadness saying, "Crying helps me slow down."

Riley is now feeling homeless within herself, which her mother and father fail to detect because they are so busy. But her crisis does not become a breakdown until the first day at her new school. She has to introduce herself to unfamiliar classmates and, standing alone and exposed, she realizes that she misses the delights of Minnesota. She cries and, utterly defenseless, the wretched moment is introjected to become a commanding complex and core memory that threatens to color everything.

The experience wreaks the kind of mayhem in Riley's soul that would be called a trauma. Joy is not strong enough to help her through the shock. Instead, Joy's secret anxiety becomes a running panic. Riley's inner equilibrium is upset, and her desolation threatens to turn into a permanent depression. Much of the movie tells the story of Joy's shifting relationship to Sadness, and how Riley's personality, not just her mood, is at risk of changing, particularly when Anger, Fear and Disgust gain free rein.

It's a powerful portrayal of what happens when someone slips into melancholy. They will not only feel low but angry and terrified, and then, at other times, full of hate and loathing. One of Sigmund Freud's insights complements Jung's, as Riley disintegrates. What can be called depression sets in, Freud noticed, when people forget that they are actually "just" sad, as a result of losing sight of what they are sad about. They have nothing to focus on and so become listlessness and unable to find energy or take pleasure. These movements within the psyche will be familiar to many.

A turning point for Riley comes when Anger steps up. This is another tremendous insight because anger is not straightforwardly a bad emotion. Its gift is that it is energetic and so can counter melancholy, for all that it can misfire. In the story, Anger gives Riley an idea. She will return to Minnesota, the place that she knew to be happy. Practically speaking, it's a bad move, but imaginatively, at the level of soul, it prompts a fascinating turnabout.

Now lost in the depths of her psyche, Joy and Sadness

rediscover an imaginary friend that Riley had when she was a younger child. Called Bing Bong, it is Riley's childish version of another feature of inner life that is acknowledged in many spiritual traditions, known as the second self or divine double. Socrates called it his daemon, a voice that first spoke in his childhood and stayed into adulthood. Others have talked of guardian angels or spirits. The key feature is that, although often hard to comprehend, they are always for us and will even sacrifice themselves for us.

As a child, Jung had one. It took tangible form as a manikin that he carved out of the end of a wooden ruler to look like himself. He hid his double on top of roof beams in the attic, an action that helped him look after himself. "All of this was a great secret," he wrote in his biographical book, *Memories, Dreams, Reflections*. "In all difficult situations, whenever I had done something wrong or my feelings had been hurt, or when my father's irritability or my mother's invalidism oppressed me, I thought of my carefully bedded-down and wrapped-up manikin." It symbolized a part of his soul that was safe from any events, introjections and the rampages of damaging complexes. It was a kind of substitute for the imperturbable presence that adult spiritual intelligence can discover, which a child will struggle to detect because it has not yet gained a resilient enough sense of itself.

In adulthood, the divine double can take on different forms and is sometimes known as the higher self or tutelary spirit. They show up across the globe from the ancestors and sages remembered in Chinese traditions and the devas of India, to the kami of Japan and the patron saints of Christianity. They are prayed to in order to call forth otherwise inaccessible resources or to offer tips and insights.

Anthony Ashley Cooper recommended a practice of imagining a divine double and what it would be like to address it, and have it address you. He thought that such a visualization helps with the self-authoring of life, as opposed simply to reacting to events or others. An imagined divine double is "a vocal mirror" that "presents ourselves in the plainest manner." It's a valuable exercise because it is so hard to be honest with yourself. "Recognize yourself!" it would say, echoing the Axial motto of knowing yourself, and it's important to imagine the second self as a divine double because that might call forth from you the part that is a "venerable sage", which the regular part of you might learn from and follow. It is a way of contacting a source of wisdom, and if that source happens to be an angel or guardian spirit, then so much the better.

The tradition refers to that part of our soul which is most directly in touch with the divine. Socrates implied as much by realizing that his daemon was a messenger from Apollo, the god whose name means "not many", or the One. It spoke to him in moments of transition, sometimes issuing seemingly banal instructions, such as turn left not right; at other times informing him in ways that were of supreme importance, such as when he was in prison awaiting the hemlock and could have escaped: do not, his daemon told him. This moment is paramount. The spiritual intelligence that he had spent a lifetime developing would prove itself, as it did. The death of Socrates was marked by tranquility, not because he knew exactly what was going to happen to him next, but because he trusted the wellspring of his being.

Riley's infantile version of a guardian spirit, Bing Bong, cannot put her in touch with this source, but the less conscious way it acts does help Joy in this moment of existential crisis. Joy notices that Bing Bong is comforted by Sadness. Bing Bong has a cry and then feels better. It is a moment of enlightenment for Joy, like a message from the gods, as she realizes that her task is not always to stay upbeat, but that she can let in other feelings too. They are not necessarily enemies. They may be transformative. Their admittance, or integration, is an advance. Sadness, in particular, is not necessarily to be fought and avoided because it can have a purpose. In Riley's case, after the terrible day at school, this is to alert others that she needs help. Crying is not always a bad thing, at all. It can prevent trauma from settling in as a core memory. It helps people get over a breakdown.

The net result is that Riley reaches out to her parents. They comfort her and, together, confess that they are sad about leaving Minnesota too. It's a reunion, fostered by vulnerability, and aided by an ability no longer to deny that they are in distress. It is a crucial moment of transition for Riley. She learns to tolerate more sophisticated experiences that can be introjected as well, ones in which Joy and Sadness coexist. She forms more adult complexes. Her soul has become capable of embracing gradations of light and shade, and that means she can find a fresh way to relate to her new home in San Francisco. She no longer feels alienated and cut off from life. Her energy returns, in the form of useful aggression as well as everyday gladness. She can continue to grow up.

This is all good. As an account of a seminal moment in childhood, *Inside Out* presents a story of what would be called successful development. If Riley's move had not gone well, it would have led, in adulthood, to the need to revisit her development. Trauma or depression, shadows or rage, would have set in, requiring therapy or soul work. However, spiritual intelligence knows something else as well. There is not only a past with which we must deal, but a deeper aspect of the present to which we can be drawn, once difficulties in the past have been seen or resolved.

## *The soul as interface*

This further dimension is crucial to get right because, without awareness of it, the risk is that the soul becomes an end in itself and, unaware of its ground, never settles. "Love is the tension between the imperfect soul and the magnetic perfection which is conceived of as lying beyond it," explained Iris Murdoch,[40] and Julian of Norwich caught the same direction of travel from imperfection to perfection, finite to infinite, when she wrote: "For as the body is clad in cloth, and the flesh in the skin, and the bones in the flesh, and the heart in the chest, so are we, soul and body, clad and enclosed in the goodness of God. Yes, and more inwardly, for all these may decay and wear away."[41] The soul is really an interior interface or transitional zone that can open onto the quiet wellspring of being. Conversely, when the soul is not regarded as a door of perception, to recall Blake's phrase, then it can become a prison. At best, it turns soul into a palace that is filled with interest but limited by the palace walls.

I think you see this happen when people become addicted to soul work – their preferred therapeutic, meditative, psychedelic or spiritual methodology which promises freedom but, unchecked, becomes a revolving door of one workshop after another. The same pattern can settle in religious circles as well. Ministers and clerics may not talk about soul work, for fear of sounding New Agey, though they will have rituals of forgiveness on indefinite repeat. They may not advise getting to know yourself better, labelling that narcissistic, though they will want to keep you requiring ministrations from a priest, or insist on a moral imperative to engage socially with the world. This is good in itself though, ultimately, soul destroying when the soul is not drawing richly on the life of the deeper spirit.

It is not that religious rites and psychological techniques are unhelpful – they are likely to be crucial: I know that as a psychotherapist. Nor is it that their proponents are automatically cynical or deluded, though they may be. The concern is that they are not seen as practices and disciplines that are secondary, often because their advocates don't have a clear sense of the spiritual commons that is the primary pursuit. It is as if there is always another stone to turn, another sin to repent, another trauma to visit, another past life to recall, in mental nooks and crannies that are numerous and often compelling. But people get stuck in them, meaning that individuals on the spiritual quest or religious journey can feel they never quite arrive.

It can happen when institutions like churches teach that God is at a distance that no one has the ability to bridge. The mystics are often onto this. Consider the remark made by Catherine of Genoa. "God is my being, my me," she wrote. "I will have nothing to do with a love that would be for God or in God. I cannot bear the word 'for' and the word 'in' because they denote something that may be in between God and me."[42] She was part of a movement, called the Beguines, that was enormous in the Middle Ages, comprised of tens of thousands of women like her, protesting in part because church hierarchies inserted demands and dependencies in between the people and God. Little wonder that nowadays, many react against institutions like churches, maybe to the extent of concluding that God and traditions like Christianity are best rejected altogether.

This move can, though, lead to another difficulty. When faith groups aren't administering the spiritual commons, the marketplace can step in, creating what Elizabeth Oldfield has called "the wellness industrial complex".[43] It is the co-opting of practices like yoga and meditation by market forces, particularly in hi-tech and start-up circles, that uses them not for metaphysical ends, but material gain. The aim is to keep employees productive by bolstering their ego against the forces of nihilism that would otherwise psychologically de-optimize and deplete them. It becomes a spirituality-lite that "severs fruits from roots and leaves you with an armful of dead flowers," Oldfield continues.

The soul needs more to open onto and settle into. It is not an autonomous entity, but exists only insofar as it receives of the divine treasure that, incidentally, longs to be known. This is what soul is in the service of. This is its purpose. The aim should be to get to know your personal soul, which is to tolerate living with who you have wittingly or unwittingly become – with traits of hate and envy, pride and greed, terror and uncertainty that crowd everyone's interiority to some degree or other – and then to allow the soul to unveil the spirit that is untouched by these flaws and failures.

This is the way I understand the Buddhist wariness of language to do with soul. It is right to insist that anything personal is transient, so that when it is taken as permanent, it morphs into delusion. Moving beyond this level of perception is a process charted in other wisdom traditions as well. Take Dante. In the *Divine Comedy*, he travels to hell not to gloat at his unfortunate contemporaries, though for a while he does some of that, but rather to directly experience the manner in which revenge and rage infects him too. Having breathed the miasma of evil and felt its vapors constrict him, he is ready to take in the air of Mount Purgatory. Here he climbs and learns that so-called sins are not to be cleansed, but converted. The pride that can fill him with shame is a form of dignity as well as vanity, and he will need dignity to stand with God. His envy can be a type of yearning as well as coveting, and he will need yearning to complete his transformation. The main work of his pilgrimage is using his hard-won knowledge of the destructive shadows in his soul to bring his soul to the light – the light being the goal. He reaches the summit of purgatory, and the edge of paradise, where his guide, Virgil, crowns and mitres him lord of his life. It is not that he is perfect, but rather that he knows himself well enough never again to fool himself, and so can henceforth manage his flaws. That is what is required to rise into the heavens. Julian of Norwich concurred. She wrote of longing to be exposed to faults, so that we "verily and truly know our own soul." This is the state of self-awareness that therapy, meditation, church-going and the like can bring, thereby enabling an embrace of the spiritual commons of which the soul is a moving image.

Jung learnt about this when, as an adult, he reflected upon his manikin. He saw that it was a child's attempt to follow an intuition, which was right, for all that he couldn't absorb its full meaning in his early years. He came to call what it represented his No. 2 personality and knew that it was of great importance. It was a bridge to an eternal reality from which springs both time and space and the contents of everyday life, externally and internally. His spiritual intelligence matured when he realized that "there existed another realm, like a temple in which anyone who entered was transformed and suddenly overpowered by a vision of the whole cosmos, so that he could only marvel and admire, forgetful of himself. Here lives the 'Other', who knew God as a hidden, personal, and at the same time supra-personal secret. Here nothing separated man from God; indeed, it was as though the human mind looked down upon Creation simultaneously with God."[44]

No one wants to be in purgatory forever, any more than they want to be trapped in hell, which is to say that no one wants to be doing soul work or penance forever. It can be intense, which brings its own attractions but, left unchecked, it is ultimately isolating. What satisfies is the abundance, freedom and simplicity which run within, through, above and under life. The sooner that can be perceived, if only in part, the better. It can then shape the purpose of any ongoing therapy, subsequent workshops and temple-going. People can then find the right relationship to the huge variety of devas and kamis, saints and sages, angels and daemons that they might otherwise be tempted to worship. They are companions, or sometimes tricksters – spiritual analogues to the friends and enemies that arrive and depart as we pass through the various stages of life.

Relating even to the most illustrious of such spiritual figures, like the Buddha and Jesus, requires careful discernment. Many Buddhists and most Christians would say that the founding figure of their path is not only a messenger, but the message. In their mortal lives, these Axial adepts embodied what they taught to such an extent that they incarnated not only the teaching but the goal of the teaching. In the Buddhist tradition that would be called Buddha-nature, a luminosity of mind that displays the paradoxical quality of being empty and so omnipresent. It is the essence of all beings. In the Christian tradition that would be called Christ consciousness, which has parallel properties of being open to all things because fully human and, therefore, an unhindered outpouring of divine life in human form. In mainstream Christianity, this dual nature is captured in paradoxical expressions such as that Jesus is the son of God the Father, as well as being one with the Father. It's a tricky business to get right, not only verbally, but devotionally. You feel it getting out of balance when Christians are infantilized by their worship of Jesus, and sense that he has become either an imaginary friend to them or a commanding officer, issuing instructions about what to do. What is missing is the unspoken conviction that they themselves can incarnate divine life, because of an awareness that their life is already a manifestation of it. This nuance is spiritual intelligence.

## *Sycamore seeds and shining*

Another Pixar movie can illuminate this awakening. It has the title, *Soul*. It combines a near death experience with the ennui of the modern world to tell a story that, like *Inside Out*, subverts self-help nostrums, but also takes the extra step of revealing what I've been arguing lies at the heart of spiritual intelligence: the felt presence of being's wide shores.

Joe Gardner is a music teacher stuck in a school with kids who don't seem to care. One day, he is unexpectedly asked to accompany a jazz saxophonist megastar, Dorothea Williams. It's a big break and he becomes so elated that he stops looking where he's going, steps into a manhole, falls, and collapses into a coma. It seems that he will miss the gig that might have made his life, though he is not dead yet. Within the coma, he embarks on a near death experience, or NDE.

He finds himself in a timeless zone called the Great Before, having escaped the stairway that leads to the Great Beyond. He does not want to go heaven, and his attempt to return to earth in time for the performance drives the plot.

The Great Before is where people prepare for life on earth. It is not quite a bardo state, as Buddhists depict the realms of recovery between lives. Nor is it being held in the mind of God, which is how the Christian imaginary sometimes talks of life before birth. Rather, the unborn souls in the Great Before are receiving the character and spark that they need to be able to make a stab at terrestrial existence. They attend "You Seminars", although interestingly, they don't have names and so cannot say, "I am Connie" or "I am Libba", but are instead known by plain numbers. I think this is an early clue as to the deeper message of the movie. Knowing who you are means being able to say, "I am Gerry" or "I am Terry". It means understanding your individuality and its links to more. The souls don't yet know how to say it and, tellingly, You Seminars don't help. Like overzealous soul work, they are focused on the wrong level.

Joe has spent his life pursuing the dream of a breakthrough in the music business. He loves jazz and has assumed that if and when he plays, he manifests his passion and gift, and so becomes himself. His goal is to make his name, which is a widespread view of life's meaning, but he starts to realize that the goal is illusory. Parallel misconceptions are called "finding your thing", or putting in 10,000 hours, ideally so as to become well-regarded, if not famous. It's a pursuit of recognition from the outside-in.

Should fame pass you by, as is fairly likely, there may be the consolation of an occasional peak experience or a steadier sense of purpose; a life organized around your heart's desire, or one featuring flow states, though we have already touched on their addictive risks. In fact, when Joe meets another character, Moonwind, from "Mystics Without Borders" – which works across reality's ontological divisions – Moonwind tells him a shocking thing. "Lost souls are not that different from those in the zone" – meaning flow states. "The zone is enjoyable but when that joy becomes an obsession, one becomes disconnected from life." Positive experiences can detach you as effectively as negative ones: the pursuit of happiness can be as disorientating as existential pain, if they are distractions from awareness.

But gradually a truth starts to shine through. What might come from the inside-out? Maybe it is about discovering a glory Joe already has? This would not be about gaining qualifications, or even knowing joys like music, though that may happen along the way. It would be about him remembering who he is at depth.

## *Educating soul*

In the story, this spiritual intelligence emerges simultaneously at two levels. First, Joe starts to realize how he is appreciated by his family, friends, and some of his pupils. Remembering their kindnesses and recognizing the love is invaluable. It warms him up for his main realization because, second, he discovers the trick of enjoying communion with others. He perceives this richness and finds it is enough because it is, in fact, everything. It is not a consolation for an otherwise frustrated innings, but is the root from which the hopes he had sprang, and it is much better to be in touch with the root than the snappable twigs and leaves that green and wither. He finds the spiritual commons that is everyone's spiritual commons. His being is the being of all.

It is an education of desire that transforms his earlier yearning for more into a recollection of the measureless nature of existence. It is an education of the mind, showing how life is not a linear path up or down slopes of failure and progress, but is a return to a presence that is available moment by moment. It is an education in the type of knowledge that isn't driven by competitive goals or chance breaks, but by a love of contemplation. It understands that the task of this life is polishing the soul's mirror to enable its shiny surface to reflect the light of heaven and earth. Joe becomes educated in the qualities of the present moment, the power of now. Something as humble as a sycamore seed, which at the peak moment of his awakening, he sees falling from the sky, is known as radiant with divinity.

Joe becomes aware of this regardless of his abilities and outside of peak moments. It's his true name, expressed in the uttering of "I am Joe", which is his to find in his life, as it is everybody else's. Joe's particularity is the means by which he participates in the universality of life, without reserve. In the movie, this theme is developed as it becomes clearer why souls come to earth. The rough and tumble of incarnate existence is the place to discover that the unchanging and infinite, the lovely and satisfying, cannot be outdone by the changing and finite, the ugly and compulsive. As some Buddhists say, nirvana is samsara, which is to say that the moment someone realizes that there is no need to escape the wheel of life is the moment they are liberated from its suffering.

Joe discovers that he has everything he needs, regardless of life's peaks and troughs. To recall the thought of the poet, Thomas Traherne: he only has to "want like a god" to perceive the world aright, which is not as a monstrous dictator, but as a creature who can affirm it all with spiritual intelligence.

### Music matters

For Joe, one of the key effects of this awakening is that the meaning of music transforms. He no longer hopes that one day he will perform the perfect jazz solo, chanced upon by a lucky combination of opportunity, skill and flow. That may well happen, but of itself, it is too transient a goal to deliver lasting peace, as Dorothea Williams explains to him in the story. Her name means "given by God", which is appropriate as she knows a better way to understand music. It is akin to the way that C.S. Lewis outlined, in a talk, not the movie, that subsequently gained the title, *Transposition*. Music exists between worlds, the Oxford Inkling explained: the physical world of acoustics, the aesthetic world of harmony and the spiritual world of vitality. It transmits a great sense of reality. Music has soul and that joins with Joe's own embodiment of life: it is a form of cosmogenesis, which is to say that it is not about making more stuff, but is about amplifying, diversifying and extending what is good, beautiful and true. It is about delighting in the abundance and freedom of the spiritual commons.

This is why ancient peoples intuitively knew to put music at the center of their rites and pilgrimages, myths and feasts. In India, it is called yoking yourself to the divine spirit, or yoga. In Greek, it is called the work of the gods, theurgia. Both can become the core around which a life is orientated. For instance, the ancient Greek philosopher, Iamblichus, developed a theurgistic method of soulful education, designed to awaken all parts of the self to its divine origins. Sometimes the awakening requires cultivating a sense of resonance with life in its material aspects: going for a walk or making a clay pot can do that. Sometimes it requires cultivating a sense of resonance with life in its less tangible aspects: listening to music or enjoying the warmth of a smile can do that. Sometimes it requires cultivating a sense of resonance with life in its abstract aspects, like appreciating the subtleties of science or the wisdom of an argument. A good life contains all modes of perception, Iamblichus taught. The core concern of the theurgy is welcoming this awareness into each, and knowing it in every part. The activities and rituals are experienced as an intermingling of the human and the more than human, and become charged, at times as if wisdom is rushing in. What was taken as primary can become secondary, so that the primary can shine through.

## Soulful discovery

Life then dramatically changes. The universal presence of the spiritual commons, channeled by soul, is responsible for the thrill of discovery. The scientist feels it when the apparently dead quantities being studied correspond to something within themselves, stirring up a gasp of recognition. The naturalist, E.L. Grant Watson, describes the experience when studying phyllotaxis, which is the arrangement of leaves on the stems of growing plants. "These illustrate a spiral sequence which conforms to a definite mathematical formula," he explains.45 It's called the Fibonacci sequence, 1, 2, 3, 5, 8, 13, 21 etc. – with the pattern on plant stems provoking awe because it is the same pattern that the mind knows as a mathematical sequence. It appreciates the elegance via math: the next number is given by the sum of the previous two. The plant appreciates the elegance because the sequence optimizes its exposure to the life-giving sun. Qualities of being are shared across the divide of conscious observer and budding leaves, which Grant Watson registered as wonder. That's soul in greater service, and it's why Aristotle called soul the form of matter, meaning the formative pattern and pulse of all that physically exists. It's visible to spiritual intelligence.

We can enquire further as this awareness is not only valuable for the wonder it brings. It can become a developed attitude towards the world and worked into a scientific method, as was championed by the philosopher and poet, Johann Wolfgang von Goethe. The eighteenth century polymath argued that the imagination plays a key role in scientific investigation because it exposes the scientist to the forces that lie within phenomena. Training the imaginative faculty helps the investigator in the process of discovery by illuminating what is, at first, implicit and buried in the life of the rock, plant or creature. In a way, all scientists attempt to peer into it, which is why they attest to moments of intuition that lead to the insights, which they subsequently test. Goethe was interested in understanding the nature of this allusive spark, and not leaving it as an unexplainable instant of magic. He does so by describing the process as scrutinizing the meaning of the existence of what's being studied, which is qualitatively different from studying it by measurement, observation or analysis. It is to enter into the shared realm of soul, from which the fullest understanding and interpretation of the natural world emerges. Grant Watson puts it like this:

> We cannot come near to life, or to the mystery of existence, by merely thinking about things. The deepest form of reality resides in life... In life we are in the presence of something which transcends material form. Life leads us into the region of what has been vaguely named spirit; by thinking about life, rather than about things, we enter into the spiritual world. The analytical, quantitative approach of modern science has barred man from the perception and recognition of the spiritual. The spiritual is qualitative, never merely quantitative.[46]

Grant Watson was writing in the 1960s and it is still taboo to talk about the meaning of existence as if that might be a scientific question. Then again, the question of meaning persistently hovers around science and an essayist like Annie Dillard will pursue it. For example, in *Teaching A Stone To Talk*, she describes a man called Larry who is trying to listen to stones speaking. It seems a kind of madness but, Dillard asks, is not this the hope which drives the scientific impulse? A meteorologist will record the wind's direction and speed, but are they not drawn to their science because they hear the wind's cry, Dillard wonders? Geologists assess the layering and age of stones, but did they not first hear the rocks call out? Cosmologists chart distant planets and stars, but is it not wanting to experience the sublime grandeur of space that makes them travel there in their minds? They certainly play up the wonderful immensity when presenting their discoveries to the public. The swelling orchestral music and gorgeous photography of a popular science show is crucial, partly because the abstract science is deemed indigestible; partly, I suspect, because the show or popular science book is a chance for the scientist to express what inspires them all along. "What is the difference between a cathedral and a physics lab?" Dillard asks. "Are they not both saying: Hello?" The soul is an important counter to Ockham's rough razor and AI's Faustian pact.

An important influence on Goethe was Anthony Ashley Cooper. He was taught by another British philosopher John Locke, whom I mention because Locke's empiricist approach to life overwhelmingly shapes how people usually talk about the natural world today. Empiricism is the idea that the only dimension of reality that is trustworthy is what we can know via our senses – not because the senses reveal soul, but because they tell us about what is most real. When a scientist or politician insists that they are following the evidence, they are parroting Locke's legacy by conveying that they are doing what is sensible and most likely to be right. It's led to a mechanical experience of life, interpreted as a complex network of causes and effects – do this and that happens – and the purpose of such knowledge is primarily to gain control. It equates science with power and views nature as a resource to be probed and plundered.

Ashley Cooper rejected this reductionism with force. He disagreed profoundly with his teacher. He felt that Locke's philosophy turned soulful living into a set of rules and doctrines. "Philosophy seems at present to be the study of making virtue burdensome and death uneasy," he wrote in a letter to a friend. His brilliance lies in seeking to recover the light and lightness of a full awareness of life.

He sought a different foundation for his convictions and found one in the aesthetic. He saw that beauty is not an add-on, an optional extra that brings color to otherwise dry laws and descriptions. Rather, it is precisely that which enables us to see those laws and descriptions in the first place. It's at work inside them, springing from the spiritual commons.

To put it another way, our intelligence is a conscious expression of the intelligence that surrounds us. So, instead of science being a means of corralling nature, it can be a means of learning to relate to it. Human beings can know that their genius and nature's genius have a kinship. They arise from a common origin. Seek the inner liberty that can't be taken from you, Ashley Cooper advised, because it is the freedom enjoyed by the sun when it rises and the bird when it flies.

### *Voyaging in the presence*

I heard an exquisite account of reaching this goal, spoken by a settled soul, who happened to be a monk on his deathbed. It opened a TV documentary called *Brotherhood: The Inner Life of Monks*, which is about the abbey of Mount St Bernard in Leicestershire, England. "I've been sixty years or more in a monastery," Brother Liam Strahan explained as he fought for breath. "In the early days, prayer was something that we did. Now, I don't pray. Prayer is the atmosphere in which I live. My whole life is just a prayer to God. You understand? I don't say prayers. The presence of God is something that I'm aware of all the time. I'm just living the presence of God. That's my prayer." He was speaking not of a romantic hope but a careful analysis of his life. He spoke with the clarity of death's timeless perception. He knew what Aristotle observed about the end of life being the moment to tell if it had been happy. Brother Liam was affirming yes, it has, even as his soul passed away. The documentary subsequently included his funeral, which was entirely right. It quietly celebrated his life, which is divine life. It was not only about bringing mortal life to a conclusion.

Many spiritual adepts can help us here. Those who have made the journey, from Shankara to Teresa of Ávila, offer guidance from a position of direct knowledge. One metaphor that I particularly like was offered by the Sufi master, Ibn 'Arabi, who deployed the notion of voyaging. He saw that any life, and any moment in life, can be described as voyaging from, to, or in Allah – the name for the being of being.

I already mentioned his insight about those who voyage from Allah, by denying the existence of this level of reality or turning their back on it. They may be making the mistake of assuming that their being is their own possession, and so cut off from being itself, when it is not. Or they may be making the mistake of thinking that they are so far from God that they are lost and aren't worthy of enjoying the divine presence, though they are worthy, simply by virtue of being alive. Alternatively again, they may be coming to a realization: although they feel that they are far from appreciating their true nature, they are actually encountering the unending reach of this awareness. The distance they sense is an expression of this vastness. Moving "from Him", as Ibn 'Arabi puts it, is therefore actually to be moving "to Him".

The second stance, which is consciously moving to Allah, can take on different misguided forms. A first is to mistake the soul for God, as I have been exploring, which Ibn 'Arabi calls "immanencing": not seeing that the divine presence is beyond as well as within soulful experience. One feature of this error is making God in your own image, as opposed to sensing how you are made in the image of God. A second form makes the opposite mistake. It insists that the creator is at a great distance from the created, perhaps because of imperfections or sin. Church teaching can imply this, as we noted before, and Ibn 'Arabi calls it "transcending" in the sense of insisting that there is an infinite, unbridgeable gulf that separates the world from its origins. An endless round of confession and penance might be one reaction to this confusion. However, there is a third type of moving to Him that is right. In these moments, the individual appreciates the value of what "arises in their interior", as Ibn 'Arabi puts it. They can move imaginatively from the outer to the inner vitality. This cultivates the soul in the way that it works best, as an organ of receptivity, because what is being recognized is that the divine light is bringing it into form. Ibn 'Arabi calls this "verification", or making true. It's the insight of spiritual intelligence.

Ibn 'Arabi continues his analysis. There are also voyagers who already understand that the soul is a means to an end, as Joe discovers when he sees that the effulgence of a sycamore seed shares the same radiance as his soul. Such individuals voyage in Him, Ibn 'Arabi explains, though there can be missteps here too. In particular, there is the tendency to rely too heavily on "reflection and intellect". This is clinging to all things soulful – the harmonies and insights, resonances and beauty, imagination and experiences of awe. No matter how creative, no matter how replete with divine reality, this delight can hinder a crucial step, which I have been describing as seeing how the soul is an interface. These joys must be passed through.

When that passing happens, voyaging to Allah is corrected and voyaging in the divine itself becomes possible. This is established in the awareness of awareness. As another Sufi, Farid ud-Din Attar captures it in his poem, *The Conference of the Birds*: "The lovely forms and colors are undone, And what seemed many things is only one." For Ibn 'Arabi, it is to be aware of every lovely form, without any lovely form being restrictive. The soul is no longer a prison or a palace but a zone of reception. "Every sensory and spiritual form is a place of His manifestation," Ibn 'Arabi writes in *The Meccan Illuminations*. "He is the One who speaks through every form, not in every form."

These realizations, in turn, must be read in the light of another key perception, which is that seeing reality in this way is seeing with God's eyes. "For none other than Him perceives Him, so it is with His eye – may he be praised! – that I see Him," Ibn 'Arabi explains. This remarkable, even seemingly blasphemous, insight is daring, though it is the same understanding that the Hindu sage, Paramahansa Yogananda, reached when he remarked that his guru saw through his eyes, because his guru was God to him and so in him, as God always is. It is the same apprehension that Meister Eckhart had when he declared that "My eye and God's eye is one eye, and one sight, and one knowledge, and one love."[47]

They are heady thoughts. They may be spoken by a settled soul. They may also be proclaimed by a monster. Jung called the latter display "inflation", which is an enlargement of the personality, as opposed to a flowering of the personality as it channels more. The telltale signs that something has gone wrong are arrogance, hubris and authoritarianism. The cult leader who commands followers, and so abuses them, provides a case in point. They are dangerous because they pretend to be divine, and may believe themselves to be so, but have forgotten that although the source of being is within us, it does not belong to anyone.

This is a crucial thought and it leads to my next step, five. It is concerned with the centrality of understanding the meaning of death. In part, this is a guard against inflation, though it is much more than that. With spiritual intelligence, death can be known not as an unfortunate termination of life, or the great enemy, but as a friend. It not only can but needs to be embraced on this path too.

## A quote
"We are always before the Supreme – cut off is utter dissolution, which would be no longer to be – but we do not always attend. When we look, this is rest, this is the end of singing ill, and we lift a choral song full of God. In this choiring, the soul looks upon

the wellspring of life, wellspring also of intellect, beginning of being, fount of good, root of soul." Plotinus, *Enneads VI 8-9.*

## *A question*

The word "soul" is routinely critiqued and mocked in the modern world, and its existence is frequently denied. And yet, Google Ngram implies that its frequency of use has not much changed over the last 500 years. Why do you think the notion of soul carries such ambivalence?

## Step 5

# Learning To Die

Spiritual intelligence has much to do with death. This is not because death is by definition a tragedy, though it clearly is sometimes. This is not because death is the great leveler: spiritual intelligence knows that the full vitality of being is what all share. It is not because death is nothing at all, as spiritual intelligence knows something else: that death is the path to life. This is why understanding the meaning of death is a central focus in many wisdom traditions – in fact, I would say it is a key focus in any wisdom tradition worth taking seriously. This fifth step is about gaining a felt sense of what is said about death and why.

It is, in fact, relatively easy to summarize. The core insight is captured in an old prayer. It says that "in the midst of life we are in death", which is exactly right, because it cannot be that in the midst of death we are in life. Life is prior to death. There is an asymmetric relationship between the two. Death cannot put an end to life.

This doesn't necessarily imply postmortem existence. In fact, some would say that the liberation death can bring depends upon there being no afterlife, because that means no one has ultimate control of their life. Death should, therefore, deflate the most monstrous ego and can also sustain the humble soul, who gives themselves to the life that they have got, like the sun blazing until it burns out, even as its radiating energy seeds the birth of other stars.

Iris Murdoch captures the dynamic in her novel, *The Unicorn*. She describes a character facing death who doesn't believe in life in the hereafter. He is a convinced materialist, and this allows Murdoch to imagine the best that such a conviction can hope for. She describes how, as he thinks inevitable death confronts him, he lets go of life and finds it to be a wonderful relief. This is what she imagines he thinks: "Perhaps he was dead already, the darkening image of the self forever removed? Yet what was left, for something was surely left, something existed still? It came to him with the simplicity of a single sum. What was left was everything else, all that was not himself, that object which he had never before seen and upon which he now gazed with the passion of a lover. And he could always have known this for the fact of death stretches the length of life. Since he was mortal, he was nothing and since he was nothing all that was not himself was filled to the brim with being and it was from this that the light streamed. This then was love, to look and look until one exists no more, this was the love which was the same as death. He looked, and knew with a clarity that he was one with the increasing light, that with the death of the self the world becomes quite automatically the object of perfect love."

It is an honorable position, undoubtedly held by many people in a secular age, at least in principle – which I say because Murdoch's character doesn't die, in fact. Instead, the sublime moment does. He survives and life returns to normal. Death returns to being its unglamorous bookends. And this is the fear: too often, a less noble attitude shapes the prospect of demise. It is a form of hedonism and regards the curtailment of life as a reason to want more from the time you have: the point of life is not to let go of yourself into a wider life but to seize the daytime of your life and all that might be enjoyed in it.

When the attitude towards death becomes a life-grab, it's disastrous. It creates a vigorous desire: to ring as much as possible from within life's limits. "How to be a success!" shout self-help books. "Get to it!" scream YouTubes. The resulting mania might be manageable for an individual, but not for a population. It can't be just coincidence that the worldview called scientific materialism, which insists that death is meaningless and that life after death is an impossibility, has coincided with the growth of cultural materialism that is consuming the world and may not be able to stop itself, even whilst it studies and measures the planet's desecration.

There was a philosophy that tried to contain this risk. Ancient Epicureanism taught that death leads to nothing at all *and* that life is not to be consumed or controlled. Its abstinent founder, Epicurus, said the goal is to be as happy as Zeus feasting on Mount Olympus when all the good Epicurean has is a glass of rainwater and a barley cake. Further, it was said that Epicurus' humility meant that the cosmos flowed into him. Material simplicity brought him spiritual freedom, as was described by his Roman follower, Lucretius, in *On the Nature of Things*: "The keen force of his mind conquered, and he advanced far beyond the blazing walls of the universe and traversed the immense whole with his mind and soul, whence, a conqueror, he brought back to us the account of what can arise and what cannot, and by what rational principle each thing has its power bounded."

The trouble is that Epicureanism is a failed philosophy. Its central doctrine, that less is more, has morphed into the precise opposite. Anti-consumerism, and a vision of life found in small pleasures, took its first adherents to lives outside of the pleasure factories called cities and into communities called The Garden. But nowadays, it takes adherents right back into the center of cities. Epicureanism implies excess, and an Epicure is a person who takes pleasure in fine wine not rainwater. That a modern Epicurean dedicates a life, presumed to be short, to sensual enjoyment and escalating pleasures implies that the problems of modern life will not be resolved without a different attitude towards death.

So, I want to turn back to the older traditions because they promise something else. They make a bigger claim. Death can be reimagined. In one way or another, your and my life goes on. Death is not the end of more but the path to more.

The older traditions say that what dies at death is ignorance about the meaning of death. This is why Jesus talked of losing life to find it, and why the Sufi, Balyani, writes: "People's existence does not disappear, but their ignorance disappears." It is why Chuang Tzu does not grieve but sings when his wife dies. "When she had just died, I could not help being affected," he tells Huishi. "Soon, however, I examined the matter from the very beginning." That "very beginning" is the spiritual commons, the originator of the coming and going called life and death, which is how he knows that his wife is now lying "in the great mansion of the universe." This is where she and he always were anyway, and to say otherwise, would be like saying that when summer dies, the seasons die. They don't. What happens when summer dies is that it becomes another manifestation of the seasons, called autumn.

## *Proving life after death*

One way of trying to see this is clearly pointless: attempting to prove that there is life beyond death. This is a fool's errand because the evidence that would count as proof would be material evidence and so reflect the dynamics of death, not life. William Blake caught the conundrum. The natural, by which he meant the empirical, can only see the natural, and will invariably "rise up against" the spiritual sight required to see more. "Imagination is the divine vision not of the world, nor of man, nor from man as he is a natural man," he wrote.[48] It is a spiritual faculty – the intuitive ability to which Plato allocated the largest part of his divided line. It sees beyond or through evidence.

Further, any evidence that was amassed would need to be interpreted, as scientific facts must be, and the scientific materialist would feel impelled to treat it as unpersuasive or, at best, inconclusive. This is why sceptics bang on about extraordinary claims requiring extraordinary evidence. It's an evidence escalator, which in the case of life after death becomes exponential. Blake called this fix the "crucifying cruelties of Demonstration": it has the tendency to make what most matters the most uncertain. It is why an open-minded and thorough investigation into life after death, as Lesley Kean documents in her book, *Surviving Death*, can only conclude that "death may very well not be the end."[49] She examines cases of purported reincarnation and finds them astonishingly compelling, accounts of near death experiences and feels they are almost irrefutable, and the communications of mediums, which are less evidentially strong because they vary hugely in quality, though may still be compelling. And yet, she ends with the question still on the table. There are always other explanations, from cognitive bias to intergenerational telepathy.

The same uncertainty haunts probably the most thoroughly examined story of postmortem survival in history, that of the resurrection of Jesus. Around 4,500 academic books and learned articles have been written on it since 1975 alone, according to the New Testament scholar, Gary Habermas. And the result of the colossal efforts of these trained historians and biblical scholars? Something happened. It might have been hallucination. It might have been hope. It might have been honest witness and testimony, but the reports are inevitably questionable.

However, Kean suggests another way forward. "We can draw our own conclusions, based on consideration of the evidence, our own experience and our sense of inner knowing and connection, all of which inform our relationship to the question of survival," she writes. I think that is correct. It is not a new observation either. Ancient philosophers noted that what counts as evidence is directly related to personal experience.

## *Leaning into death*

The older wisdom is to treat death as an opportunity to reflect on life. It is to bring the two close together, not see them in opposition. Moving towards death, as mortal life inevitably does, can reveal – not rationally but experientially – that the deathless embraces mortality.

This is the approach that Plato adopts in his dialogue, *Phaedo*. It is one of his accounts of the last days of Socrates and is the most dramatic because it ends with Socrates dying. There are two other dialogues, which cover different facets of his passing, so Plato's aim is clearly not to present evidence. Rather it is to offer reflections that might reveal the inner significance of the moment.

In the *Phaedo*, the scene is the prison, with Socrates on death row. He has been there since the judgment of the Athenian jury and his sentencing. He has not yet drunk the hemlock because of a religious festival during which the city mustn't perform executions. The wait has been hard. One of his followers, Crito, had tried to persuade him to pay a bribe and go into exile. Socrates had refused and now the festival is over. The moment has come.

His family and friends surround him. Some are scared and upset. Some of them cry. Others want to discuss practical matters, seeking distraction as an aid. Proximity to death does that. It raises all sorts of reactions. It catalyzes anxiety and makes fears obvious. Plato deliberately sets them before us. He wants us to feel the moment, not merely read about it. This is a first step to seeing whether deeper truths about death might emerge.

Socrates is the focus for that possibility. All eyes are on him as the one closest to inevitable death. The tension mounts because one certainty rules the drama: Socrates will be dead at the end. That certainty forces the great uncertainty the dialogue is about: the meaning of death, if it has one. It asks us whether we, as readers, with the comfort of not actually being in the cell to face the fateful moment, can stay with the tension, to tolerate it. The implication is that the seeming opposition between life and death might shift. It might give way to a third, unexpected intuition.

Socrates says that the route he wants his friends to follow in these final hours of his life is akin to entering the Cretan labyrinth.

The issue is not whether there is a death-dealing Minotaur at the heart of it, because there is. The issue is whether, like Theseus, he can face death and overcome it, not with Odysseus-like brute force and cunning, but by resolute commitment.

His strategy is not to seek an argument that might trounce all counterarguments. Nor to offer a story of admirable courage that will blast away all doubt, though the death of Socrates has been presented that way in art. Rather, it is to head directly towards the doubt but with an open not closed mind. He has realized that by paying closer attention to death, which is what he has been doing during his life as a philosopher, subtle truths reveal themselves, not because he reckons he knows what happens but precisely because he doesn't. It's a bit like what people can report when they have been with someone who dies. At the end, approaching the precipitous moment, fear fell away. It looked like a departure, not a termination. They can't say what that means but it gives them pause. Might what appear to be horizons turn into the crests of hills? Might what seem like exits turn out to be ways in? That said, the significance of these intimations can only be contemplated by staying with death as it happens, which is what Socrates asks his friends to do. "You yourself" are the opening words of the dialogue. They ask us to accompany him as he dies.

The tension necessary to perceive death aright is only discovered as the tension about death rises inside ourselves. It builds as our props and beliefs, distractions and hope, fall away. The proximity of death dissolves them, leaving us with nothing we ourselves can maintain. That is the truth of life, which death reveals. We don't have it. It has us. Ultimately, we can't control it, secure it, command it, indefinitely prolong it. The question, then, is what we make of life's origins? Where does it come from and how is it sustained?

It is time for Socrates to lean into his deepest and most tested intuitions, as he commits his life to the hemlock. His followers can emulate him, if they commit to the experience with him.

## Dead ends

That's the setup. The action begins with Socrates as he removes his chains. It's a custom of kindness offered to the condemned on their last day. He stands up, rubs his legs, and remarks how amazing it is that pain can so quickly be replaced by pleasure. But then he chuckles: it is not amazing at all. In life, pleasure always follows pain, as pain follows pleasure. The one rises as the other falls. They are like twins conjoined at the head, as if two sides of the same coin of experience.

The implication is that death might be viewed similarly, as if it attends life, as life attends it. Or maybe it can be viewed differently, by detecting a rhythm that is not determined by such a mechanical ebb and flow. It's a first different thought and nudge towards an alternative perception.

Socrates' companions listen in. He tells them that he has been having dreams in which a god told him to sing a more beautiful song. He understands it as a challenge to philosophers, he continues, who can easily sing the same song time and again. They come up with arguments, and tease them out. They derive implications and knock them down. But is this all that philosophy can hope to achieve, a never-ending cycle of rational propositions and equally rational rebuttals?

This repetition is pretty much all that philosophy has become, Socrates implies, alluding to the sophists of Athens – and possibly to what he suspected philosophy would become, when consumed by logic and obsessions with coherence, and thereby abstracted from the raw experiences of life. It would amount to little more than a defense against life's tensions, which are easier to deny with the hope that they can be dissolved by reason. Only, it is hardly surprising that such an activity can't make much headway when it comes to the ultimate questions. Abstract reason does not know what it is to die or live.

William James is one philosopher to see that this is precisely the predicament that philosophy has reached in the modern period, and that it requires a corrective. He called his suggestion "radical empiricism". He meant that the most direct evidence must be included in any discussions of issues, which is first person experience itself. The psychologist in him also knew that this takes time to recover. It is possible to become entirely ignorant of what is going on most intimately and directly within you. A person can be almost wholly unconscious as they pass through the business of the day, especially when that is supported by a culture that does much the same. "Only as reflection becomes developed do we become aware of an inner world at all," he notes.

Psychotherapists know it. Having done a philosophy PhD and worked as a psychotherapist, I've concluded that the practice which originated with figures like Freud and Jung is closer to ancient philosophy than modern philosophy, for precisely this reason. Modern philosophy doesn't ask you to work on yourself, when working on yourself was the wellspring of insight for Socrates and his companions.

Freud repeatedly refers to Plato as "the divine Plato", and both knew that change happens when listening to the soul, the inner vitality of life, detected within the body, not when only listening to the head. Experiences of hope, aspiration, fear, doubt are particularly detectable when death is near. They rise involuntarily to the surface, rather than being concealed in secret in hearts. So the last day of a life is a good moment to attend to them. It is a good day for philosophy. And Plato's dialogue lays all that before us. He describes what happened to Socrates' friends and what they said.

Some hoped that the soul is separate from the body and so capable of floating off at death. Not if a soul is to the body as the music is to a lyre, Socrates replies. No lyre, no music. No body, no life.

Some became puritanical and ascetic, as if the best way to find eternal life is to beat the desires and hungers of mortal life into submission. But, remarks Socrates: to want life by treating much of life as revolting or unclean is a contradictory and self-defeating approach.

Others decided that the best way to deal with mortality is to amplify life whilst it lasts, as if turning up the volume might screen its end. It is possible to seek fame or fortune, and worry about a legacy, hoping a kind of timelessness is gained by being remembered. It might be, though fame inevitably fades and flickers as well, Socrates points out.

Others again decide to cultivate virtues so as to know that which is most beautiful, good and true. If life is to leave them, then at least they will have known the best of it. This is close to the path Socrates had chosen, though might it too turn bittersweet? He can know that his followers will testify to him being the most honorable and admirable person they ever knew. They will speak of him amongst themselves. But if death is the end, then death is also the beginning of the end of any glory. The body that perishes would be a prison even for the loveliest soul.

## Prison's portal

The mood in the cell chills. Darkness creeps across the minds of the friends. Is death going to defeat the genius mind of Socrates? Are his thoughts really a death knell? Is his song fading and dying?

There is a crucial, aching hiatus in the discussion. The friends of Socrates feel the full force of death's challenge, as they must. They must know the failure of trying to argue it away. If they felt they could reason themselves to comfort, death would lose its potency to point to more. They would squander its alchemy. They would not be exposed to what they cannot control and see what that might offer to them. And sure enough, at this point in the dialogue, they worry they have reached a horizon over which they cannot peer, and that they are looking at death as the ultimate limit. In the telling, Plato has Socrates engineer the concern. He magnifies it – because that might, in fact, help. There are other possibilities that they must test and abandon, and see what truths are left. Death is a moment to let go.

Remember too that Socrates is not a materialist. He is not talking about life as something purely mechanical. He knew about such a view. His life as a philosopher had begun by being drawn to it. The predecessors to the Epicureans had promoted a new type of physics because they thought they could explain everything that happens in the world as a seamless chain of cause and effect. The hope was that matter bumping into matter, like tumbling boulders leading to an avalanche down a hill, could account for everything – from where we find ourselves, to where the stars are in the sky; from how the weather works, to how society works.

However, Socrates had been unpersuaded and, at one point in the *Phaedo*, he explains why to his friends. Ask yourself, he says to them, why I am in prison awaiting the hemlock? He explains:

A strict materialist would have to say that it's because my legs moved in a certain way, when I walked through the door, and my brain fired in a certain way, when I willed my body to walk. That's part of what happened but it's far from all that was going on prior to my imprisonment, and is certainly not the cause of it. That would be the Athenian judiciary finding me guilty, which is to say that justice and morality are the reason I am here. They are bigger than my life and there's something bigger than them I am prompted by as well: my commitment to what is good and true.

In other words, he knows his body to be the tangible expression of his soul, which he knows, in turn, to be an interface to the immortal. This is his everyday experience. His spiritual intelligence sees that his whole being rests on the spiritual commons. Death, therefore, can be befriended as a way in which he knows his consciousness shares in the consciousness of the gods, because our being and theirs springs from, and returns to, being itself. We don't own life, life owns us.

He invites his friends to detach themselves from identification with their embodiment, not by turning from it, but by understanding it more deeply. Know yourself, had long been his motto. It is not failing him now. The conversation picks up again.

## *Seasons and cycles*

Does this life you describe not follow cycles, someone asks? Is it not like the plants that sprout and flower, wither and die, only to sprout and flower again? Does it not move through moments of being hot and then cold, like the weather? Are we not a manifestation of embodied life and so like all others, which are born, grow and die, only to be born again? Why would we regard our life as any different from the many forms it takes in nature?

There is a more abstract appeal to this reflection as well. If life and death are part of a cycle, that doesn't require something to come out of nothing, as if the person we are sprang into being from nowhere, self-caused. Something cannot come from nothing, unless what looked like nothing was something already. So, the implication is that the beginning, middle and apparent end of our life is actually one turn in a much longer, perhaps unending, cycle. They are contemplating the transmigration of souls and the possibility of reincarnation, which was a belief in Plato's circle.

It is a comforting thought, though only for a moment, because death could still enjoy a victory, Socrates muses. It might consume all that is distinctive about a particular life, which would be the person we know as the individual of that cycle.

We might still disintegrate, unless something is passed from cycle to cycle, much as parents pass characteristics and features to their children. But still, parents are not their children. The memory of a person still perishes. The individual still dies.

There is a second hiatus in the discussion. The light splutters. The atmosphere darkens once more. Death has become more palpably present – which means that something else comes into view.

## *Eternity in time*

After all, Socrates continues, do people not report detecting what's timeless in time? They experience eternity in the here and now. The transient can convey what's unchanging, like the beauty that shines from within a breathtaking bloom, or the perennial truth that lies within an intuition. Does not the fleeting carry meaning because meaning is not fleeting? Love and intellect are as such. They reach into us and reach out from, as if transporting us to another realm. Do they not reveal that there is, therefore, a divine part in us? Mustn't it be so that only the eternal can enjoy the eternal, meaning that we can enjoy eternal perceptions because we are eternal too?

This is the point at which the light of their conversation shines most brightly. It's much like what I've been exploring here too. Spiritual intelligence alerts us to the deathless, inexhaustible spiritual commons. For a moment or two, it seems as if Socrates and his friends have seen through death. They feel the deathless directly within themselves, a bit like a mystical experience. They contemplate its palpable presence between them. A god seems to be among them.

But then Socrates bursts their bubble again. Maybe the timeless returns to heaven, when the body returns to the earth? Maybe we are allowed to be containers of divine intuitions, but only for a season? Maybe we are not like the gods and need a body to experience what the gods know without embodiment's mediation? What the gods give, the gods can take away. Once more, there is nothing they can cling to.

They feel death's absoluteness anew. The time when Socrates must drink the hemlock is near now. In terms of the dialogue, we readers are two-thirds of the way through. There are fewer pages to go than the ones that have been read, the book in our hands itself mimicking the fall of the sand through the hourglass of time. Plato appears to be wasting much of it, if there is to be a rabbit pulled out of his philosophical hat. Is the death of Socrates going to be doubly devastating because the hour he spent before it, he spent failing to overcome it? The labyrinth continues to look like a trap.

Socrates pauses. He tussles Phaedo's hair. The youth after whom the dialogue is named is handsome. Is Socrates saying goodbye to what is lovely? Is he seeking comfort?

## *Friendly death*

He is not. He is releasing what is not timeless and seeing if anything is left. And Phaedo inspires him. He turns to his friends once more. We have been missing something, he declares. The worry about death concealed a truth that hid in plain sight. Put it like this, he suggests. What matters is not that we can't agree about what the soul is, or about the meaning of life's cycles, or about the timelessness of timeless perception. What matters is that we know to contemplate them at all. Of course, we mortals can't fully grasp what is immortal. We wouldn't be mortal if we could. What matters is that we keep longing for and loving it. We would know death had won were we to stop bothering about what is eternally true and good.

The failure of their arguments is precisely what they need, he continues. Death teaches us not to try to see around it, to see under it, to see over it, but to keep going towards it. And then see what survives. The apparent collapse is really a clearing for a truth to shine through, which may be the main purpose of death. The point is that we don't have life, any more than we have a summer's day or a lover's embrace. They have us. And giving up the delusion – getting the relationship straight – is crucial. When we achieve that, something else comes into view. Life is bigger than death in the same way that it's bigger than us. This is what it means to be a philosopher: to see that the soul, whatever it might be, receives its vitality from what holds us all day, every day in life – being, consciousness, bliss. The paradox is that sometimes this perception can only become clear when we think we're about to die.

At this point, with the transition called death moments away, Socrates has never been clearer. He submits to the radical empiricism that sees through whatever would separate him from the most intimate awareness of life. With death near, it has strangely never been easier. Life and death: the two stop appearing to be in opposition. As he greets death, as he knows it directly, he knows that what many say about it was only half right. Death clears away, yes, but it clears away all that is not wholly, blazingly, intimately life. It is in life's service. We will see more than we ever have before, right in the face of death.

Death's revelation has been portrayed by the novelist Leo Tolstoy, which he describes in his famous story about someone dying, *The Death of Ivan Ilyich*. It tells of an antihero who had lived an empty, bourgeois life. But as his mortality becomes undeniably real, all that he owned, all that he valued, and all his vanity, burn away. That leaves exposed a radically different, entirely unexpected perception of life. It is one that he didn't know existed at all, because he had presumed that he understood all that existed. In his nakedness, clinging no longer to anything, he finds infinite space, the spiritual commons. "He searched for his old habitual fear of death and didn't find it," Tolstoy writes. Then, with his final breath, an entirely unexpected question comes into his mind, which he could only ask at that moment: "Where was death?" Tolstoy portrays Ilyich stepping towards a wider life. "What death? There was no fear, because there was no death. Instead of death there was light." Death enables him to see it.

Not all of Socrates' friends are convinced, which is only to be expected because what he is conveying can only fully be known when death has become a welcome companion, and everything else has been let go of. For some, perhaps most, that will only happen when death is unavoidably close, although Socrates wants to nudge his followers in that direction before that happens. He belongs in the tradition that teaches it is possible to die before you die, which is to say, to become familiar with death in mortal life. It's why Plato wrote the *Phaedo*. It's why I've tried to write about life and death in this way here. The practice showed Socrates something during his life: it is possible to hold to what is good and true regardless of what happens. If you do, there are things that no one can take away from you, including death. Socrates' deathday confirms it. He had been dying to himself every day of his philosophical life and now, finally, with actually dying, he is stepping into that which held him all along: the source of life, the sustainer of his love, the teacher of his agency. He never saw it more clearly than he does now. Death is his guru.

The inevitable happens. The dialogue draws to its end. Phaedo reports that Socrates died beautifully and calmly. His mortal life ceased, but he had seen more. Life is not a moment in death. Death is a moment in life.

In Christianity, the reorientation of awareness of death as the enemy of life to being seen as a bearer of life, is described as losing your life to save it. In Buddhism, it is the goal of discovering no-self. In Indian philosophy, it might be talked about as sacrificing oneself to the greater self, called Brahman or Krishna. The philosophies vary in the details. They speak the language of particular times and cultures. But a shared insight can be seen threading its way through them all, which is what you would expect were it true. Plato conveyed the same.

## Death and transformation

If you bring death into life, it becomes a bringer of life and dissolves the boundary between this life and whatever happens next. This is the practice of dying before you die, and it used to be widespread. I once gave a talk on death at the Tower of London and was given a tour of the former prison cells. They are packed with often beautifully carved skulls and skeletons performing death's dance, the danse macabre, inscribed onto the stone walls. "Don't worry. You'll soon rejoin us," the jiggling bones might say. These prisoners were reconciling themselves to their fate by contemplating how it might be their liberation. They could sense it with death so close.

The graffiti looked similar to the traditions that encouraged contemplating death in Tantric Buddhism. Statues show various gods in symbolic and often ferocious guises walking on corpses, representing aspects of what must die in order to find life. It might be that what we would now call the ego must submit, or that death must be approached to understand why it need not be feared. "If one hears this Tantra [meaning religious text] and, understanding it, holds to it and performs the recitation all the time, in this lifetime all fears will be washed away," promises one god. The powerful tension between life and death is cultivated in these meditations. It has the ability to transform the perception of life, though must also be practiced carefully, for fear that the anxiety overwhelms a student.

In the Christian tradition, the link between anxiety and insight is known as the tropological, from the Greek tropos, meaning turn. The phrase was coined in the centuries following the death of Jesus, at first to aid the reinterpretation of Hebrew scriptures which might illuminate the meaning of the recent events, and in time to develop the notion of conversion. The idea is that realization does not come with literal understandings of life, because they will be ones with which you are comfortable and familiar. Nor does it come with moral demands, which might question what you are doing or who you are, though as often as not leave you feeling guilty as charged. Real change only comes with a breakdown or crisis or fundamental disturbance. That may require an unflinching and seemingly brutal exposure to the reality of mortal life, though only so as to reveal the spiritual commons that offers life itself.

A brilliant expositor of this way is William Blake. The very energy of his verse and images might immediately prompt the suspicion that this is a writer who is not merely hoping to explain or illustrate but revolutionize understandings. He wants to tip you off balance, so that a new balance might be found. He seeks release from "mind-forg'd manacles" and also what he called "Eternal death", by which he meant the naturalistic understanding of life, as complex biology, that has already excluded the spiritual ground from which life comes.

A tremendous experience of it was offered by the exhibition of his work at Tate Britain in 2019. The show was enormous, including three hundred of his works ranging from his now most famous single plate, *Ancient of Days*, to the breathtaking illustrations of Dante's *Divine Comedy*. Some critics thought that the scale of the display was too much, but I felt it caught the essence of Blake's purpose. I was glad of the experience. Its magnitude prevented me from trying to sort Blake out and put his wild images in the tidy categories of my mind. Like the freedom of a dream, be it troubling or ecstatic, the gift of the show was to immerse you in his vision and sight, and see what it stirred up.

It's often noted that Blake was fond of polarities, and their juxtaposition can achieve the same effect. Heaven must be married to hell, he taught, and his illustrated books don't offer designs that straightforwardly unpack the poetry, as if saying the same thing in visual form, but rather set up oscillations between the verse and the pictures. The imagination is dared to enter a third domain that's related to what's perceived, but isn't allowed to rest there. "Attraction and repulsion, reason and energy, love and hate are necessary to human existence," he explained. His method is to present opposites in the hope that they penetrate surface appearances and offer glimpses of a fuller life. What's familiar dies in his mythological universe. The trick is to run with the energy, much as the trick with a dream can be to allow its scenes to continue after waking. There's no right or wrong; no mere fantasy. Amplify the feelings and resist the reductive tendency to explain, which only explains away. Blake writes: "I give you a golden thread, Only wind it into a ball, It will let you in at Heaven's Gate Built in Jerusalem's Wall."

That quote comes from his epic poem, *Jerusalem: The Emanation of the Giant Albion*, in which a Christian inspired version of tantra can be felt unfolding. Blake takes us on a virtual journey of exposure to different states of mind, be they good or terribly destructive. All states can be felt as he leads us across four domains.[50] The first is Ulro, which, when seen with clear eyes, might give way to Generation, then Beulah and, finally, Eternity.

He characterizes Ulro as single vision. "In Ulro, that which can't be expressed quantitatively does not exist," writes the Blake scholar, Susanne Sklar.[51] The Ulro state of mind trusts reason and numbers alone, and any confusion is met with the cry to gather more evidence. It's experienced by the subterranean Newton, to recall another of his best-known images, whose devotion to measurement closes down other forms of awareness. Alternatively, and to recall his vision of the sun, an Ulro-mind can only see it as guinea-form. It will conclude that the sun is best described as an average star, in an average galaxy, nowhere particular in the cosmos – which is itself regarded as a vast void of mostly empty space.

Ulro produces a weary life. It turns living into a "dull round", with the thought of death being bewildering and meaningless. But the despair can deepen into a collapse, which can then become a tropological turning point, and Generation appears.

This state of mind has twofold vision and gains its name from a newfound interest in reproduction in Blake's time. In Blake's poetry, the character of Los is often in this state. He swings his tongs and hammer, tools that can forge and create, not merely measure like Newton's compass. He labors to build the city of Golgonooza, a flawed utopia or restive city on earth. When it comes to the sun, people in Generation will remark that they are made of stardust, acknowledging that in their nuclear furnaces, stars like the sun forged the building blocks of life, such as carbon. They will discuss whether an average sun is about right for the genesis of biological life. It's a modest, mental upgrade in the appreciation of our celestial companion. There is a bit more life in it.

Generation is more expansive than Ulro, although it still lacks spiritual intelligence. The nagging sense that life should offer more therefore means that there's a constant risk it slips into pursuing reproduction for reproduction's sake – mere replication: generation, not regeneration. That can become pathological, falling into what Freud called a repetition compulsion. At a social level, it produces escalating consumption because of the insistence that death is a bookend and no more. Things can fall out of control and obsessive habits set in – though with the crisis, there can be a chance to see more again. Threefold vision can break through.

This is the mindset of Beulah, in which life is known for its richness and soulfulness. Feeling and ardor, sympathy and happiness, and above all, love, come to the fore, refashioning the narrower states of mind with a wider vision. Rich seams of meaning and value, aspiration and hope are uncovered, to the extent that people in Beulah intuitively know what it means when life is said to be in touch with the spiritual commons.

Spiritual intelligence has been born, and poets will pen lines to the blissful sun, couple it romantically to the moon, and praise its warmth and light for falling equally on all. Some may detect intimations of divine blessing within that pattern. However, the spiritual intelligence of Beulah is still limited.

In particular, death is regarded as a tragedy and that might bring out a dark side when the love of life, which is felt intensely, becomes a desire to possess and control it. Death will be felt as the enemy. Dylan Thomas' famous poem caught the mood when he spoke of raging against "the dying of the light". It's a dangerous state of mind. It wants what the spiritual commons holds, and feels it may be close, but hasn't yet the mature spiritual intelligence fully to know it. However, if Beulah can learn from the rage, and not to be merely consumed by it, a further conversion becomes possible. A freer participation in life and another lifeworld may start to be anticipated: Eternity.

Eternity trusts spiritual intelligence without reserve. In Blake's language, what achieves take off in Eternity is fourfold vision: the realization that perception can open onto infinite life. Space becomes fractal, time fluid. Julian of Norwich testified to the change when she wrote of how her "bodily vision ceased, and the spiritual vision remained in my understanding. And I waited in reverent awe, rejoicing in what I saw."[52] Eternity abides in nothing less than divine life, and an ingenuity that isn't only spectacular and fun, but generative and lasting. As Blake's contemporary Samuel Taylor Coleridge put it: fancy rearranges what it already knows, more or less arbitrarily, often just for effect, whereas this type of perception synthesizes, makes, closes the gap between the subjective and objective, and is aware of the interior vitality of the world as well as the multiplicity of forms it takes in animals and plants, seascapes and landscapes, skies and stars.

Life is known to be primary and so death becomes a gateway to fuller life. Because death requires a letting go, it brings the individual to a moment, "borne on angels' wings," Blake wrote, that is a threshold. It is traversed with what he called "Self-annihilation", the mental fight with oneself that isn't about dissolving the ego but routing the desire to command life. Another perspective emerges, too, because death is seen as not only a teacher looming ahead at the end of mortal life, but as a guide who is always present. "Every kindness to another is a little Death," Blake writes of this realization, because kind acts are sacrificial. They can be experienced by the giver as moments in which to realize that they never possessed life to start with, and so the life we have been given can constantly be given away. This is practicing dying before you die: we live because life pours itself into us, and the best response to that is to pour it back out, as an offering or gift. When people do this together, the nature of being alive is revealed as a "comingling" of mutual self-sacrifice. The giving and receiving precipitates "Fountains of Living Waters", which flow, unlike the cisterns within which even Beulah had tried to hold onto life. For Blake, the Christian, the meaning of Jesus's death, and ours, is revealed as part of this ongoing resurrection. In Eternity, the everyday deaths through which we pass as moments in life come and go, reveal that there's a source of life that is perpetually giving. It is a timeless love, which includes and transcends death.

## The nature of self-sacrifice

That said, this notion of self-sacrifice is readily misunderstood. It easily slips into masochistic forms of self-abnegation. Blake's brilliant quatrain gets the meaning right.

He who binds to himself a joy
Does the winged life destroy.
He who kisses the joy as it flies
Lives in eternity's sunrise.

Blake's point is that this is a type of sacrifice that leads to more, not less, mirroring the dynamic of death opening onto more life.

The text that first gave me a sense of what this entails was not in fact one of Blake's, but one from another tradition, Indian philosophy, though it turns out that the same text had a major impact upon Blake too. I am thinking of the *Bhagavad Gita*, which Blake read and thought should be much more widely known across the Christian world. He references the deity Brahma in his poetry, liked the meaning of "gita" as song – a poem that transforms by accessing spirit – and even drew a portrait of the *Gita's* translator, Charles Wilkins. "Blake was among the first of the European idealists able to link his own tradition of thought with the *Bhagavad Gita*," explains Northop Frye. It seems that his sense of emanation, in which all things flow from a universal source and so partially reflect it, came from the *Gita*. The song also explains how the empirical senses see only a portion of the soul that is connected to the aboriginal spirit which fills and refills the spiritual commons.

The *Gita* is set at a moment of unavoidable, seemingly deadly calamity, the day on which the warrior, Arjuna, faces his foes in battle. That would be bad enough, though his foes are also his brothers. Arjuna breaks down at the impending slaughter. The thought of the bloodshed makes him weep, though his breakdown thins the barriers that exist between mortals and immortals. The proximity of death again brings a horizon into view, over which Arjuna finds he can see. Immortality in the form of the god Krishna appears to him. They converse.

Krishna fosters an inward turn in Arjuna, which brings the realization that death is best not argued away, but embraced, because of the inner truth it reveals. Much as Socrates discovered, it is that life has us, a fact that we know most deeply when we don't try to hold onto it. In the case of the *Gita*, the way to develop this insight is via the intention with which life is lived and actions are performed. As the inner meaning of each moment becomes clearer, a subtler awareness of life takes root. The process is captured in one of the repeated insights of the text, the necessity of acting without desire or concern for the results of any action. "For it is through acting without attachment that a man attains the highest."

It is thought about in relation to sacrifice, with self-sacrifice emerging as the way of bringing death close to life so as to open onto more life. It is another practice of dying before you die. It has a range of specific characteristics.

The aim is not to focus on benefits or results but rather to cultivate a sacrificing attitude. In the terms of the *Gita*, this means offering all that one does to Krishna, or back to the infinite life from whence all came. In the terms we have been using here, this reorientates the sacrificer to the spiritual commons that does not change. It is an inner sacrifice, a continual flow of receiving and releasing, that allows the individual to get out of their own way and know reality as it is.

It is the opposite of clinging to or searching for security, which has a specific term in Indian philosophy, of non-attachment: "Treating alike pleasure and pain, gain and loss, success and defeat." Another short verse from Blake captures the attitude:

Man was made for joy and woe;
And when this we rightly know,
Thro' the world we safely go.

And this can be learnt: it's sacrifice as a practice that becomes an art of living and lived sourced of wisdom about life. It is a form of radical empiricism. In time, activities come to be experienced as free from specific desires and intentions and so full of "the fire of knowledge", an expression akin to the cosmic consciousness spiritual intelligence detects. It is an offering of oneself that cultivates a dis-identification with oneself, though does not simply deny the self either. Rather, it is a holding lightly to light – kissing the joy as it flies – and so dying to specifics and the tendency to assume I am, or you are, this or that. It is to know Blake's fountain of living waters and Plato's intuition that death is a portal.

At Arjuna's moment of crisis, he has little or no perception of the inner meaning of things. His sign is the monkey, the symbol of an unstable and so unknown mind. He is operating exclusively at the concrete level when he faces his brothers, believing he must slay them or be slain. His mistake is believing that performing his duty as a warrior consists in performing in a certain way. What he glimpses is that letting go as he acts is to learn to see more than his actions, which is also to see more of reality itself.

Self-sacrifice might be summarized as the difference between a sacrifice made for human ends, and sacrifice as a realization. It's sacrifice as a form of knowing rather than achieving. As Shankara explains, in his commentary on the *Gita* that became seminal in the development of nondual Advaita Vedanta, that's because sacrifice as knowledge is not aimed at results. Instead, it's aimed at opening, so that more of life can be said yes to, regardless of what it brings. It is a path of expansive awakening. The Gita calls it "remaining absorbed in consciousness itself", which can be glossed as identifying with the spiritual commons, in the light of spiritual intelligence, rather than the identities and personae of our mortal life. It is then possible to become "a knower of reality".

You can go so far as to say that the *Gita* presents self-sacrifice as the primary activity of mortal existence. It puts learning to die center stage, and so is another core wisdom tradition which understands the right relationship between death and life. To use more theistic language, it is to seek to align one's will to God, to surrender will to God, and so to live in God and know God's presence without and within. It holds out a vision which shows that the inner meaning of sacrifice is that the life of sacrifice is life known to be divine.

It is a simple approach to living – using "simple" in its richest sense: a singular stance or way of life that reveals all. And again, it can seem disturbing. In a way, it has to be, and those who say it is not are probably revealing they have not understood, because the disturbance is what tropologically opens up eternity. Marguerite Porete was also onto it. In *The Mirror of Simple Souls*, she portrays the voice of reason worrying about whether this can really be true. What does it mean to insist that there is a way of living that gives up willing? What is being said if there is a perspective from which poverty isn't distinguished from riches, ease from disease, love from hate, even hell from paradise?

Porete has the voice of love answer reason's concerns because, when it comes to the critical junctures when a genuine conversion might occur, love is a good guide – the selfless love that gives up its own claims and generates a kind of disinterested desire and curiosity. Porete stresses that this kind of insight can only be understood when it is actually lived, so the risk of stepping towards it must be taken. "No scripture teaches it, nor can reason comprehend it, or the travailing of deserts reach it," Porete writes. "But it is a gift given by the Most High, in whom this creature is lost in knowing, and becomes annihilated in her understanding," she adds.

We have been looking at the profound, revelatory links between death, life, letting go and self-sacrifice. That has led to the old practice of dying before you die, that can take the form of small acts of kindness as well as turning towards seeming calamities. It answers the ultimate question of the meaning of death, not with a proof but with a revelation: in the midst of life we are in death, not the other way around. However, the path to that awareness is demanding. To appreciate what it means in its entirety, means offering up all that you have, love and appreciate. The promise is that much more will be discovered in return because you will live with much more than you could possibly own. Intimations of unending delight will replace hedonism's accumulation of passing pleasures. A pathway to life's all provides an alternative to the consumption of more and more, for fear of life's limits. Infinite horizons appear with the collapse of tunnel vision.

Learning to die brings a revolution in terms of living and awareness. It could hardly be more radical, and will seem foolish to some, fearsome to others, and to others again a full, unrestrained response to the precipitous moment that the modern worldview has brought us. And there is more to say about that now as we turn to another important pivot that comes with step six.

### A quote
"Deception is not as creative as truth. We do best in life if we look at it with clear eyes, and I think that applies to coming up to death as well." Cicely Saunders, magazine article, September 1988.

### A practice
The Buddhist practice of tonglen, from the Tibetan meaning "sending and taking", treats every breath as an opportunity to take in whatever is happening, with the in-breath, and let go of whatever is happening, with the out-breath. The Buddhist teacher, Pema Chödrön, describes it as "ventilating our prejudices", in a discussion of the practice in her book, The Places That Scare You.

It can be used in several ways, one of which is practicing the understanding of sacrifice explored in this chapter. Have a go right now. Breathe in to savor what's happening. Breathe out to sense the space in which everything is happening.

## Step 6

# Resonating With Reality

There is one type of death which is eternal that William Blake identified. It is not imposed from without, as if a law of inevitable mortality or the revenge of a capricious god. It is sustained from within, by mortals. It's an all-consuming shadow that can sweep over humanity, evacuating meaning and growing with the assumption that life is nothing but complex machinery, coupled to a few illusory side effects like consciousness. The conviction is as deadly as a dissection because it restricts the imagination and encloses the spiritual commons by insisting that existence is, at base, marked by survival and struggle. It rules that spirit is superstitious and that intelligence languishes in isolated minds which must gaze out at the darkness. It judges Homo spiritualis a fiction for the muddle-headed.

But much as life embraces death, so light can always penetrate the darkness, and the nihilism that runs so deeply through modern culture has prompted a backlash. The philosopher, Mary Midgley, noted that the reductive trend in biology has left the science in the untenable position of claiming to be the study of life whilst being "life-blind", and so unable to incorporate into its models fundamental facets of creaturely existence, not least of which is the buzz of being alive. Even humble insects display quirks of character and signs of desire if you take the time to look, and networks of fungi show remarkable cognizance, as the biologist, Merlin Sheldrake, has pointed out in *Entangled Life*. Alternatively, the emergence of twentieth century physics, which is wholly unlike what came before, led innovators such as Werner Heisenberg to state the self-evident: scientific materialism is "obviously too narrow for an understanding of the essential parts of reality", he wrote in

*Physics and Philosophy*. Those essential parts for him included mind, soul and God. Whatever they might be for you, they can't simply be discounted as delusions.

What's deluded is to fall in awe of machines. An AI, say, can solve all sorts of problems, like recognizing faces by spotting patterns in the data, but spiritual intelligence has the ability to recognize that the human face is a mirror and reflection of a lively, vulnerable soul. It is not just an object to manage by tracking its movement around the city. It is the tangible manifestation of a person, who may be anxious about their identity, concerned for their future, or thinking about how delicious the pie just purchased will be to eat this evening, when shared with another person whom they love.

The philosopher, Ivan Illich, put the challenge in this way. The problem is when methodologies and devices compete with human flourishing, as if they might be the important element themselves. They catalyze a pruned, disenchanted worldview. They cease working for us and we start working for them, under a promise of increased efficiency. Illich worried that education has ceased to be the activity in which we ask about the good life as it has become the activity of adapting to the next technological iteration. He feared that people's desire to learn, drawn by the delights of wonder, has become a weary need to know, cowed by a terror of tomorrow. Reductive approaches are not inherently bad, he stressed. The question is whether we are crafting ways of life that are hospitable to our humanity, or harming it. And reductionism does harm it when we forget that we are radiantly alive.

Blake affirmed the same. In the climax to his poem, *Jerusalem: The Emanation of the Giant Albion*, he sees Francis Bacon, Isaac Newton and John Locke, who stand for the geniuses of the sciences, joining hands with John Milton, William Shakespeare and Geoffrey Chaucer, who stand for the geniuses of the arts. They have things to teach each other and, when they do, perceptions of reality are precipitated that are way bigger than any of them imagined. Blake celebrates "the innumerable Chariots of the Almighty" appearing in the heavens, as the arrows of their intellects fly joyfully across the sky. It is this capacity to resonate with reality, across all its dimensions, that we will turn to now.

It matters because I think we have become traumatized. For an individual, a trauma is something that damages or destroys a part of them. Bearings are lost, and the day is filled with anxiety, bubbling up like an oil seep, in a variety of debilitating ways. The same can be said to have happened, or be happening, at a cultural level. Nietzsche famously named the modern trauma, the death of God. He imagined the loss being announced in a marketplace, which has replaced the temple as the organizing principle for society, and has the news proclaimed by a madman. It takes a madman because humans are doing what a mad god might. "How could we drink up the sea?" he cries. "Who gave us the sponge to wipe away the entire horizon? What were we doing when we unchained the earth from its sun?" The prophet continues by voicing the vertiginous experience. "Are we not plunging continually? Backward, sideward, forward, in all directions? Is there still any up or down? Are we not straying as if through an infinite nothing?" In states of trauma, everything appears to race towards exponential complexity, and existence presents itself as a continuous succession of intractable problems that resist resolution.

I stress the predicament because, like facing death, traumas can be healed when it is appreciated that they are serious. Then, over time, it's possible to question the past, so as to uncover a sense of identity and a center that can be trusted, before recreating a life from the inside out. It is a two-step movement of withdrawal to recover and return to remake, that has parallels in spiritual traditions. It's remembered in the legends that surround the Axial figures. The Buddha left his palace. Jesus entered the wilderness. Lao Tzu abandoned court life for a hermitage. Then, their failing lives diagnosed and understood, they returned with a teaching, inspired by a new vision. That remaking is our next step, given a different story, center and vision has been found in steps one to five. And at the heart of this next move, I suggest, lies the cultivation of virtues. In a way, what we can do is add more in response to Alasdair MacIntyre's second question: what am I – are we – to do?

## *Defining virtue*

The answer is to be virtuous. But can't you immediately detect a problem? The word itself. Virtuous. It means good but also prudish. It implies clear-mindedness but also holier-than-thouness. It conveys admirable qualities and ones that we may want, but also characteristics that are a bit too wholesome and cloying. It feels like it might invite you to abstract yourself from the mess of life, when in truth it does exactly the opposite. Its worth is that it is not worthy. So how can we get that across?

I think we've almost just got to live with it, though I have experimented with the Francis Spufford option. In his book, *Unapologetic*, he drops the Christian word "sin", which he feels has become irretrievably mixed up with trifling naughtiness like eating chocolates. Instead, he talks of "HPtFTU", which stands for the human propensity to fuck things up. Applying that technique to virtue produces the opposite dynamic: the human propensity to love what's good – HPtLWG – and, personally, I think that is a more powerful dynamic in the human psyche than sin. If it were not, Homo sapiens would have long ago spiraled out of control and truly ruined itself. There is hate and greed and envy in the world, for sure, but there must be just a little bit more care and love. That tips the balance, which is why, at least as a species, we live to see another day.

There's a deeper point to consider here, though, too. The virtue equivalent of HPtFTU would not be the human propensity to love what's good, but the good's commitment to not let us go, GCtNLUG. That follows from what we've been contemplating about the relationship between life and death. Life wins. Similarly, so does the good. It is what Iris Murdoch called the "sovereignty of good". It's a gentle but irresistible quality of the spiritual commons that works not by insisting but simply by being there. It draws like the sun. We live to see another day because each day the sun rises again. Sooner or later we will realize that we can sit down in it. So I am going to use the word, virtue, but every so often add GCtNLUG, as a reminder of this quiet, unfailing strength.

Virtues are habits and traits that, by accident or design, orientate a person around what is good. Conversely, vices are habits and traits that, by accident or design, disorientate a person because sight of what's good has been lost. Virtues connect to the spiritual commons. Vices flirt with eternal death. Virtues resonate with reality. Vices skirt the void. Virtues enable a type of intelligence, felt in the way they expand the awareness of being alive. Vice is a kind of ignorance, which may intensify experience but only because it narrows and excludes. Virtues are in us because of GCtNLUG, the good's commitment to not let us go, and that can be detected everywhere and in everything.

## Morality's muddle

Virtues are qualities rather than rules, and so offer a way of proceeding that is very different from conventional morality. The latter is generally portrayed as a set of ethical guidelines, or way to calculate the consequences of actions, which may or may not succeed in shaping behavior, and often distances people from existence because they foster living by abstraction. Do this! Don't do that! They invite you to imitate the haloed, not immerse yourself in complicated and possibly highly informative incidents.

You see the failure of morality in the way that the morally

worried mull over the right thing to do: sometimes they will feel good because of the way they act, frequently they will be haunted by guilt or inadequacy. You see it in the way the morally duplicitous work out how to stay dodgy whilst looking good enough. They will tick the checkbox requirements of a moral code and implement the requirements of the latest ethics committee – which is itself mostly reacting to the inconstant crowd of public opinion – signaling that they have become virtuous. But, at heart, they remain unchanged. Sooner or later, most people become demoralized by such cajoling, unless they are cynical or bad, in which case they will do the cajoling and appear to thrive. In a typically punchy manner, Blake called it "the Wastes of Moral Law", because the approach wastes life, much like intensive farming wastes land. Another way of putting it is that morality does not understand GCtNLUG.

Ultimately, morality is a dead end, which may sound alarming, until it is recalled that it has only been around for a couple of hundred years. Immanuel Kant argued for a morality based on musts and oughts at the end of the eighteenth century, and Jeremy Bentham invented utilitarianism in the nineteenth. Their success was to eclipse virtue ethics, which had been the main way of thinking about how to live well since at least the Axial Age. Kant and Bentham pursued its demise because, in different ways, they sensed the death of God. They had become disillusioned about the ability of humanity to resonate with reality and be drawn to it. Kant thought "the thing in itself" lay over a rainbow that can never be known directly. Bentham thought that any intelligence besides his mind was likely a fiction.

## Evolutionary psychology

Virtue ethics is making something of a comeback, much like reenchanted science, though often in depressed ways. I say depressed because qualities like altruism or trust are typically discussed via the science of evolutionary psychology. It treats virtue as a means of survival, which undermines what philosophers from Aristotle to Al-Ghazali stressed – that virtues are excellences and ends in themselves. This is because they are direct manifestations of the good's commitment to not let us go. Dropping GCtNLUG, and replacing it with evolutionary struggle, depresses the peace and contentment virtues might bring.

Further, there is a thread of fatalism in the science, claiming our behavior is hardwired into us by the conditions of life tens of thousands of years ago. "Sociobiologists believe, quite generally, that how altruistic any organism is, towards another of the same species, depends on the proportion of its genes which the first shares with the second," explains David Stove in *Darwinian Fairytales*. As his title more than hints, the book was written to undermine such notions. Incidentally, it was recommended to me by a professor of evolutionary biology from a university that, the last time I looked, was at the top of the science league tables. Agitation for change is coming from many directions.

Skepticism of evolutionary psychology arises because it offers silly explanations for why, say, parents devote their lives to their children. In this case, it's called kin selection. This is the logic that someone loves their children because their offspring share half their genes.

I might be inclined to regard such fables as actually abhorrent, not only silly, because my family includes two adopted siblings, and I can tell you that sharing no genes makes no difference to the sense that we are brothers and sisters. Further, as a psychotherapist, I know that a child's life can be ruinously destabilized by a parent who was more devoted to their work or garden or pet than their offspring. If genes were so determining, that would not happen nearly as much as it does.

Of course, there often is such a thing as parental altruism. The problem is when altruism is explained in such a way that it is explained away. For example, equally impressive as self-sacrificial parents are self-sacrificial saints, like Florence Nightingale, Elizabeth Fry, Abbé Pierre or Maximilian Kolbe. But evolutionary psychology presents them as anomalies, not exemplars who might inspire us with their fuller humanity. Stove continues: "If your biology makes a 'problem' out of the very existence of such people – as sociobiology certainly does – then what that shows is that there is something wrong with your biology: not that there is something wrong with those people." Quite the opposite. Those people knew GCtNLUG.

The more technical way of putting this is that genes are taken as causative not correlative. Every scientist knows the difference and yet it is astonishing how much the confusion shapes debate. Genes certainly play a part in the way human evolution has inhabited social and spiritual niches. However, as systems biology increasingly implies, by considering factors that influence organisms from the top-down as well as bottom-up, that is because genes are shaped by, as much as shaping. Living is not a cost-benefit analysis all the way down, another idea that has skewed the popular imagination and must assist the general demoralization. Evolution is an intricate process of co-creation by discovery. It's an unearthing of reality through and through that can explored intentionally and voluntarily, which is why Nightingale, Fry, Abbé Pierre and Kolbe are rightly celebrated.

Sometimes, the collapse of the complexity of human motivations, in the name of science, reaches the level of farce. Then, it may well be better just to laugh at what is presented as gospel. Take "gorging gene theory", the proposal that our DNA still thinks we are living on the scrubby savannah, not around the corner from a well-stocked supermarket, which is offered as a way of explaining why we struggle not to binge on chocolate and sweets. It's a farcical suggestion because life on the savannah is also described as a hunter-gatherer paradise, with copious food stuffs hanging from shrubs and trees. The prevalence of food in that era is the reason that Yuval Noah Harari describes the agricultural revolution, which came later, as history's "biggest fraud".

"Moral enhancement" is another case in point. It illustrates not contradictions in evolutionary psychology but wild oversimplifications. The idea here is that hormones, as opposed to genes, cause moral behavior, so an oxytocin spray should make someone more generous, or titrating serotonin would reduce levels of anger. Apart from the mechanization of morality, what is overlooked is that generosity and anger are more than one thing. Generosity may spring from feelings as diverse as compassion or dutifulness, frivolousness or elation. Anger may be a sign of murderousness or love, righteousness or terror. It's sometimes said, quoting one of the founding figures in sociobiology, E.O. Wilson, that humans have "Paleolithic emotions, medieval institutions, and god-like technology", when surely, it's the other way round. We have long had god-like emotions, seeing heaven in a grain of sand, but now have spiritually primitive technology, which is why people retort: "That's not heaven. You're just having a hormone hit." William James had a good quip against that one. Maybe atheism is just a liver disease, he said.

## Virtue's way

This gets us back to the advantages of virtue ethics because it befriends such complexities. Confusions, uncertainty and mistakes are crucial because, as Aristotle explained, learning how to live well is akin to learning how to loose an arrow to hit the target, whether it's windy or calm, whether you're walking, running or riding. Falling short is not a sin or failure but essential for learning.

The importance of this process, with its ups and downs, was highlighted by the psychotherapist, Donald Winnicott. He observed that moral systems steal from people the chance to develop, by imposing on them a default package of right and wrong. The soulful aspect of our humanity, for which Winnicott used the psychotherapist's name, the psyche, reacts against this intrusion because it loves and is drawn to life. The psyche wants to engage with difficulties and delights on its own terms, so as to feel the ways in which it belongs to the fabric of being and can relate to the spiritual commons threaded within it. That living awareness is important for its own sake, almost – if not completely – regardless of mistakes.

Conversely, when people are denied the chance to explore their creativity, they feel depleted. The psyche longs to grow, which means being able to affirm light and shade because it has seen them, not because it has been told. The old sense of the verb "to know" is worth recalling. It implied union, not being informed about. The person who has learnt in this fullest sense is the person who knows that they are participants in, not observers of their lives.

Such a development is more likely to go well if guided, particularly by myths. They can embrace moral complexity and convey how life might be navigated, as opposed to merely controlled. Much as the myth of Inanna was a journey through life and death, and the myth of Odysseus showed the texture of freedom and craftiness, so nowadays psychotherapists employ modern myths. The story of attachment between a parent and child is one with immense utility. It tells a tale of the crucial felt connection that we depend upon in our earliest months and years. The devotion of a parent feeds us psychically, much as the food they provide feeds us physically. Winnicott summarized it in a number of pithy aphorisms. "There is no such thing as a baby." "When I look, I am seen, so I exist. I can now afford to look and see." "The good-enough mother" – who is a parent who can messily survive the intense aggression, "antisocial tendency" and "nuisance value" of their child. The messy bit is important because it shows the child that whilst anger and hate exist in the world, so does love, and it is greater.

I call this account of attachment a myth because, whilst it is not without empirical evidence, its practical value in the therapy room lies in providing words for experiences rather than a route map of development, from dependence, through independence, to interdependence. When held loosely, not rigidly, which is one of the great advantages of myths, attachment theory provides a tale against which our inner states can be assessed and understood.

## The immeasurables

There is a further related point, too. Trying, trialing and testing is valuable because virtues are not just useful, though they are. More significantly, they disclose reality. They lead to wider discoveries, via the dynamics of discomfort and tension I have called the tropological, thereby unveiling the good's commitment to not let anyone go. "Know that there is a station in spiritual insight where, when a person reaches it, he really sees all that exists is interconnected, one with another, and all are like one animate being," wrote Al-Ghazali in *The Alchemy of Happiness*. Similarly, in Confucianism, virtue, or Te, discloses the universal, all-reaching Tao. And in Buddhism qualities like mudita, or joy, don't just bring happiness but awareness of "the immeasurables".

Plato's intuition was the same: all virtues are one when seen aright, as they are responses to reality's fundamental simplicity and the sovereignty of good. You know it as you detect virtues in virtuous people. They will not be perfect, but they will tend not to have one good quality, like hope, without another, like equanimity, also being present. It's a reason virtuous people inspire others. Figures like Greta Thunberg or Malala Yousafzai are not without their faults and can't simply be imitated. Instead, they can catalyze virtuous qualities in others, manifest in those others' idiosyncratic and specific ways. The virtuous say "be more yourself" rather than just do this or that.

There is a warning needed here, which was made by Iris Murdoch. An intimation of unity can be easily confused with a troubled desire that all be in unity, which is not a true perception but a wish. It is a defense against the fear that reality may be meaningless and fragmented, and so a belief without potency – which is why, as Murdoch bluntly put it: "The madhouses of the world are filled with people who are convinced that all is one." You feel the same unbearable worry when people effusively share expressions of love in an effort to secure consolation. "Almost anything that consoles us is a fake," Murdoch added. She was exaggerating but so as to warn off a degeneration into "vague mysticism".[53]

That said, when it comes to virtues, they do appear to be universal.[54] Whilst they adopt many specific forms in different cultures, which can be understood as diverse human responses to the good, six core qualities are ubiquitous, and are also found throughout the writings of philosophers and sages from China, India and the Western world. They are wisdom, which is about rapport with knowledge; courage, which is about embracing what it takes to flourish; humanity, which is about relationships with human and nonhuman others; justice, which is about the project of living socially together; temperance, which is required to stay on a path that embraces mistakes; and transcendence, which is about recognizing these forms of life are not individualistic or solipsistic but connect us to wider actualities. All six develop the individual on the one hand and, on the other, awaken them to what lies around them. Personal development is awareness expansion, which is why virtues bring knowledge, as well as shape behavior and deepen character. Aristotle said that these elements come together to reveal "the best thing in us", which is the origin of our being, rooted in the spiritual commons.

### *Beyond self-obsession*

Virtues also square the ethical circle of aligning self-concern with what's good for others. "It is primarily by working on our own character that we become able to treat others well," explains philosopher, Tom Chatfield.[55] This creates a ripple effect because, if I see a virtuous person, I might quietly say to myself, "I want more of that." The good is opening me up. It's why successful civil rights leaders don't have themselves to be perfect. What they need is a dream that they can communicate and project, and an awareness that what really inspires others is the good. It's not that they're gods but that they channel.

There are those who argue that virtue ethics doesn't need this extra dimension and, if it does, so much the worse for virtue ethics. For instance, the philosopher, David Hume, was inclined to call virtues "monkish", or dour. He argued that they really serve a baser instinct of needing to feel the approval of others and avoiding social opprobrium. All virtue is virtue signaling. Other critics are not so skeptical. They suggest that virtues can be useful because they help you become the best person you can be, by improving characteristics and habits. A virtuous person is someone who understands the checks and balances between wanting but not wanting too much, or between their rights and the rights of others, and is happy occupying the mean. They are portrayed as model citizens, friends and lovers.

This is the worthy understanding of virtues and I think the approach is mistaken. It's too rational and forgets GCtNLUG. We are invited to love and reflect what's perfect, not be sound or sensible, and spiritual intelligence illuminates why. The soul knows more. There is a spiritual commons that radiates a sense of and taste for the infinite. The person cultivating virtues detects it and wants to absorb more. That's virtue's energy and appeal. It's sometimes called having a moral compass, a kind of inner detector for what feels true and beautiful. Anthony Ashley Cooper developed the modern way of talking about this intuition as a mode of sophisticated, inner alignment. "Tis not a Head merely, but a Heart and Resolution which must complete the real Philosopher," he wrote. He was convinced that if you learn to see the world expansively, to join in with its artfulness and dance, then you are not only more likely to make good ethical choices but to enjoy life by experiencing it in all its fulness.

Nature shares these qualities of elegance, simplicity, self-sacrifice and beauty. A felt participation with its vitality reveals its virtues, which is why naturalists and explorers talk of having respect for the world they step into. Plus virtuous behavior brings its own rewards. The insights it unfolds are not ours alone, but shared and real, coming from the good. Virtues connect in the thrilling way of being taken outside of yourself. They enable you to want the hard experiences, as well as the pleasurable moments. Trust what beautifies life and life will become beautiful to you, Ashley Cooper concluded, a motto which he put to the test. He suffered extensively from ill-health during his life. He knew difficulty, and died young, aged 42. But virtues linked him to what's true.

## Listening to the heart

This is to say that the link between virtue and knowledge has practical implications. One means of cultivating them was developed by Ignatius Loyola, the founder of the Jesuits, though he had a hinterland too. Before his saintly flourishing, he aspired to the bloody and glamorous life of a soldier, until he was gravely injured. While recovering from the brutal surgery that followed, which included sawing off bits of bone without anesthetics, he turned to reading to find succor. Some books told the tales of heroes and their noble deeds. Others spoke of the saints and their brave lives. He noticed that when he read about knights, he was amused but felt no lasting benefits, whereas when he read about good people, he was interested and felt strengthened within himself. He worked on a reflective technique that discerned the different qualities.

The sense of tranquility or expansion he called consolation. The sense of shabbiness or weariness he called desolation. The difference is felt in the body and takes practice to distinguish well, which he concluded was because he was not only listening to his heart, but was learning to reorient himself around the communications of God, experienced via the felt impact of the stories. The communication is experienced as a movement of soul and spirit. If I do this, he asked, in what direction am I travelling? The issue is not straightforwardly about doing right and wrong, though that might play a part, and can also be applied to activities that a rule-based morality would disregard as irrelevant. For example, after Ignatius had recovered, he retreated to a cave and let his hair grow wild. It felt like a good way to face his vanity. Then, a few months later, he decided that cutting his hair was best. It was not that he suddenly cared about his appearance again but that a new question had presented itself: were his spiritual exercises still productive? He decided they were not, so they must change.

Such flexibility, without loss of clarity, is specific to the moment and question at hand, which points to another characteristic of virtues and spiritual intelligence. Both resist generalizations. It's why the good advice of one day might be bad advice for another, and summary rules tend to confuse as much as guide. With virtues, what's sought is shrewdness, not diktats.

To be courageous, for example, will vary hugely according to circumstances, even minute by minute. It might mean plunging into a battle over the truths of evolutionary psychology, retreating from the heat, or assessing the most effective way to engage. Aristotle recognized the complexity of true bravery, and why it can only be learnt by making mistakes that develop a feeling for it: "So the courageous person is the one who endures and fears – and likewise is confident about – the right things, for the right reasons, in the right way, and at the right time."[56] His use of the word "right" is striking because it echoes the Buddhist Eightfold Path, which is also about learning right qualities from the inside out: right view, right resolve, right speech, right conduct, right livelihood, right effort, right mindfulness and right union. Laid out like that, it seems convoluted, but that's because the heart of the matter is the whole person you are becoming, not the list of functions you tick on a check list.

The resistance to generalizations extends to statements about the nature of things, which might be true in one instance and false in another. Whether the ego is valuable, or an obstacle, is one that you might have heard discussed. The truth is it can be both and neither. It's valuable when it enables you to wake up. It's an obstacle when it prevents you from waking up to more. It may be neither when you have woken up.

### *Focusing intention*

It's also why nuances like intention matter. Simone Weil defined intention as the just and loving gaze that disinterestedly discerns. With it, the difference between self-sacrifice as life-giving, and as soul-destroying, can be differentiated, and the life-giving attitude pursued. Intention will be alert to background noise, and whether that is colored by joy and willingness or duty and shame.

The Buddhists call this assessing the "skillful means". The Buddhist philosopher, Nagarjuna, has become known for toying with seeming contradictions, recognizing they are invitations to see more clearly. "The nature of things is to have no nature; it is their non-nature that is their nature," he writes of a quality of things – or is that non-quality – summarized in the term "sunya", or empty. By that, he didn't straightforwardly mean nonexistent, but rather having an existence that depends on how one thing relates to other things. This means that things can shape-shift because, what we take to be their reality is, in fact, a reflection of their relationship to other things and to ultimate reality, the spiritual commons.

This also helps to explain why expressions of ineffability are common in spiritual traditions. That which is ultimate reaches beyond description but can be known, much as the experience of riding a bike or listening to music reaches beyond description but can be known. "The Tao that can be spoken of is not the constant way," is the famous opening line of the *Tao Te Ching*, before continuing: "Always rid yourself of desires in order to observe its secrets. Always allow yourself to have desires in order to observe its manifestations. These two are the same." It is not a riddle. It is a pointer. It's the same with the five ways, or *viae*, that Thomas Aquinas derived for aiming the mind towards an awareness of the divine. Noticing patterns in nature, the fundamental source of things, and what does and doesn't change, won't work when treated as proofs. The noticing may work when treated as disclosing features in the fabric of reality.

Spiritual intelligence is like that. It is part cultivation, part encounter, part receiving – part embracing, part letting go, part letting in – and when the related movements are operating well, the individual feels they are ascending a virtuous spiral towards a higher, or is that more intimate, perception which otherwise eludes them. GCtNLUG. It's the tropological transformation that Blake called fourfold vision, and knew could lift us through the states of mind he termed Ulro, Generation, Beulah and Eternity. The goal of virtue is, therefore, not focused on right conduct but wider consciousness – which is why the truly virtuous don't talk about being virtuous but loving life, or just getting on with it. Their lives appear supremely worthwhile, and the opposite of worthy. I reckon that the Good Samaritan would have been shocked at the way his story has been used to preach moral imperatives. "The point of my action has been missed," he would be insisting. "I had a realization! Look! Everyone is our neighbor! Everything is one!" See that, and then do what you will. A new world might be born, not just a momentarily better version of the current one.

One example of this I feel particularly alert to is in relation to transhumanism. The word was first coined by Dante to describe his transformation when rising into the heavens in the last part of the *Divine Comedy*, the *Paradiso*. For Dante, that included a completely new vision of some of the elements that we have been considering, such as that death may be a friend not enemy, and that vices are a kind of ignorance and virtues a sort of knowledge. But transhumanism now has been perverted by technology. It has come to mean enhancement not transformation, and is assessed in terms of longevity, mood and cognition, not sacrifice, realization and beauty. Blake would have immediately spotted that the reinvention of transhumanism works to trap people in Ulro or Generation, and blocks off Beulah and Eternity.

## *Against solutionism*

The Greek philosophers called the unitive state of awareness fostered by the virtues, eudaimonia, which means "good-godedness": the state in which the sovereignty of good is loved and acknowledged. The word is usually translated as flourishing or happiness, but what good-godedness lacks in catchiness, it makes up for by conveying more precisely what they had in mind. Virtue opens us to the world around, above and below. It is not just about us, and whether we are doing the right or wrong thing, as morality would have it, before launching us on another round of worry. Rather, virtues bring about a sense that there is you, what you are experiencing, who that involves, and where that is leading.

Ask, "what is this?", over and over again, advises the writer Dan Nixon, following the teachings found in Zen.[57] He points out that, in the age of digital technologies, the question has the advantage that it hinders the rush to find solutions, as if life were a set of difficulties to be overcome. That's the preferred approach in a technological age because technologies treat everything as a problem to be solved, much as someone with a hammer treats everything as a nail. But such "solutionism" brings about the paradoxical situation in which people are caught in continual rushes of mad activity, trying to fix things, whilst everything basically stays the same, with better graphics, heightened responses, more statistics and exaggerated chaos. The reason for this disguised stasis is that technology ensures that life is viewed through the one frame, its frame. Remember Blake's Newton, leaning over a scroll, compasses in hand, unaware of the flow of life around him. As the philosopher Martin Heidegger observed, when considering the nature of technology: it doesn't just offer a way, it predetermines the way on offer. Conversely, virtues improvise multiple ways of being, held together by the good.

## *Identity politics*

Consider the discontent that revolves around identity politics. Cancel culture or keep culture? Remove statues or re-label statues? Trans rights or wokism gone mad? Where do you stand? Alternative positions seem excluded when it comes to these intense disputes, which inflame public debates over everything from gender identity to national history. Only, there are alternative responses, which spiritual intelligence understands.

A virtue ethics approach would start with the observation that all identities are necessary failures. Male or female, gay or straight, black or white, and so on: they are all attempts to secure a place in the world, drawing on anything from biological particularities to historic suffering and inner yearnings. As such, they are worth respecting. They mean much to people and matter within certain domains, such as the medical, the psychological, the social. However, it's a mistake to idolize them, as if any specific description of a human being could be the defining feature of who they are. Life can't be contained by these identities, for all that they in part shape it. The human individual is both "infinite in faculty" and "quintessence of dust", as enormous as truth and as passing as a flutter, said Hamlet. You can be both at once, and trying definitively to nail down who you are, is like trying to nail down water.

Spiritual intelligence understands recalcitrant excess as an unavoidable part of being a human person that is, in fact, positively to be affirmed because it points to something else: every human being's fullest identity lies elsewhere. It's in the dynamic ground of life itself, the emptiness or dance, the ineffable and beautiful, which moves between the different aspects of ourselves – across the corporeal, the intersubjective, the soulful – and arises from, and in death returns to, the spiritual commons.

Attempts to capture this true self in words inevitably fail, which is why phrases like "true self" are rejected as mistaken or inadequate. Socrates picked up on this difficulty, and made it central to his philosophy. As we saw, he realized that his wisdom rested not on what he knew for sure but on the fact that he could know nothing for sure, particularly when it came to himself. He made ignorance a virtue. It sounds like a curse, more like submitting to darkness than light. But it is a blessing. Not knowing who you are means you are always open to more, and this is the point at which virtues come into their own. Qualities like courage and love, trust and humility, enable us to tolerate the enigmatic nature of immediate reality, and that everything you say about yourself is provisional, because that awareness enables you continually to draw on the felt source or generous wellspring of life's ceaseless vitality. This matters because life goes well when resourced by the underground spring and, conversely, things go wrong when it gets cut off. It's why Carl Jung highlighted the decisive question for we humans, the living descendants of Homo spiritualis: are we related to something infinite or not? It's also why culture wars tend to bind more than liberate: fear of being incorrect can trap us in smaller lives.

Virginia Woolf reflected on such dynamics in her essay, *A Room of One's Own*. She begins by arguing that women are limited because they are like people who go fishing in the stream of life, only to be told that they are not allowed to stand on the riverbank. Their place is controlled by others, who are often men. The thought fuels awareness of how women are disadvantaged, to the point of being thwarted, which leads her to assume the sexes are distinct so as to be opposed. There is obvious reason to reach for this conclusion, though, as her thoughts unfold further, she sees something more, and that gives her pause. There is a downside. A world in such a conflict forces all people to live with "sex-consciousness", and this is depleting, possibly fatal, because it means that no one's minds can be freely open, or aspire to the cross-fertilization of ideas that don't just fish in the stream but plunge into its tremendous current. Then, something else happens.

She looks out of the uncurtained window from her room and across the street, and it seems that there is a lull in its usual, busy activity. Simultaneously, she notices a leaf falling from a plane tree. In an instant, all seems still and quiet. "Somehow it was like a signal falling, a signal pointing to a force in things which one had overlooked," she writes. Like Joe seeing the sycamore seed dropping to the ground in Pixar's *Soul*, Woolf's leaf falling from the plane tree precipitates a new state of mind in Woolf, that Blake would say comes from Eternity, and it makes a difference. She notices something transformative and subtle that happens next.

### The androgynous mind

As she continues looking, two people meet on the corner of the street, a man and a woman, and they get into a cab. The sight has the effect of easing the conflict with which she had been wrestling as a result of overbearing sex-consciousness, and she has the presence of mind to ask why? It was as if, previously, she had been in some kind of strain. That strain, she discerns, must arise from having to hold inflexible distinctions, in this case to do with a presumed opposition between the sexes. Such contraries are illuminating in some circumstances. Woolf wrote about them in the same essay. But holding onto them takes effort because, if maintained as ultimate, they interfere with an underlying unity, with which the sight of the man and the woman meeting had resonated and so revealed.

She argues that this unity is perceived by an "androgynous mind", one formed by a fusion of what, according to the times, would be called masculine and feminine virtues. It's a blended type of awareness that moves beyond identities and categories, becoming "resonant and porous" insofar as the person doesn't need to make the world witness to their suffering and yearning, troubles and difficulties. Woolf has the realization that there's more to being human than conflict analysis allows and, when in touch with that more, the mind is free to range across increasing circles of experience with less and less impediment. A single sentence from the pen of a writer with an androgynous mind, she writes, "explodes and gives birth to all kinds of other ideas, and that is the only sort of writing of which one can say that it has the secret of perpetual life," she continues. It's what a room of her own, practically speaking, would enable her to develop. But in the struggle to secure one, she mustn't lose sight of the broader vision, which is the struggle's point.

The sceptic may say that celebrating the androgynous mind, and insisting on the provisionality of identities, is all very well, but what about justice and rights? An answer, Woolf advances, is to engage the practical and spiritual simultaneously. The practical is the issue at hand, with all its urgency and heat. The spiritual is the developing awareness that all identifications with this or that sense of self, whilst necessary in one way are, in another, constraints. They risk cutting us off from the remarkable characteristic of human awareness: it can transcend itself. It can observe what's happening whilst it's happening, and realize that position as itself a state of mind.

This awareness is not an optional extra. It is one of the virtues of transcendence that enable us not to get stuck on one side of a struggle, but to stay free to catalyze real transformation. What seems generally lost today is that human beings can be richly resourced by the unexpected wellsprings to which the virtues can lead us. A part of us is more than ourselves and more than this world – GCtNLUG – which is also, at once, our home and the fullest source of identity. This dimension is necessary for real change to come, in my view. For example, it is striking that Woolf wrote her essay, originally delivered as talks, almost 100 years ago, and that sex-consciousness seems more disabling than ever. I think it's because over the same period of time, spiritual intelligence has declined, and the unity of mind of which she spoke is more inclined to be ridiculed – perhaps deemed inherently patriarchal. But were Woolf alive today, she would invite us to see more, I believe. Watch for the moment when a plane leaf falls from a tree. Look at how stress eases when people convivially meet. Cultivate virtues of the androgynous mind.

## Impossible forgiveness

Another virtue is required for the possibility of virtue's return: forgiveness. It must be active in the mix of qualities at our disposal because we need to be free to learn from the mistakes we make, and not be immediately condemned by them. The stance of the psychotherapist informs me here. In effect, when someone comes to see me, I say to them: everything is forgiven, whether it happened to you or you did it. Now, let's try to understand what happened and what's happening now. It's a virtue of cognitive humility.

It is much easier said than done, for the reason that was spotted by C.S. Lewis. "Everyone says forgiveness is a lovely idea, until they have something to forgive," he mused. If you finished off the Marmite, I could forgive you because I only momentarily mind. If you posted a review of my book, roundly condemning it in every possible way, then I'd struggle. And it's easy to imagine situations far worse. It's not that forgiveness is tough, or takes time, or tests our generosity of spirit, or teases us with its promise of a future free from the pain of the past. Rather, plain and simple, forgiveness might become impossible. It seems, further, that there are not only some things that cannot be forgiven but some things should not be forgiven. A list of names immediately makes the point. Hitler. Mao. Stalin. Pol Pot.

The ambivalence about forgiveness can be detected even in figures whose virtues inspire us. Take, Nelson Mandela. It's striking that commentators on his life, even those who knew him quite well, seem unsure whether he forgave his oppressors, or rather sought a pragmatic reconciliation with them. A quote of his did the rounds in the period after his death: "Let bygones be bygones," and what was often missed was what followed next: "Let what has happened pass as something unfortunate but which we must forget," the great man continued. But forgetting is not the same as forgiving.

Ancient religious systems recognized the problem by turning not to forgiveness but the practice of sacrifice – not self-sacrifice, or sacrifice to satisfy god-kings, but ritually killing animals and, in some times and places, people. Its logic, according to René Girard, is that it breaks cycles of vengeance by offering a scapegoat. It's an attempt to minimize future slaughter by making a symbolic sacrifice that acts as a spiritual or cosmic reset. The act of taking an innocent victim, and killing it, is about performing an act in order that worse acts might be halted. The sight and performance of a special death might prevent more deaths.

It's a powerful, primitive logic and persists even in supposedly enlightened cultures. Modern political philosophers have argued that state violence is a necessary evil in the world because forgiveness is not enough. Thomas Hobbes spoke of the "war of all against all" unless we submit to the Leviathan, that is governments with a legitimate power to kill. Or there is David Hume, who was honest enough to confess that if he had to choose between being able to scratch himself and preventing the world from being destroyed, there was a part of him that would go for the scratch. Desires, from minor itches to all-consuming needs for vengeance, are hard to deny.

## The long haul

A person who powerfully understands impossible forgiveness is Marian Partington. Something happened to her that would seem impossible to forgive. In December 1973, her sister Lucy disappeared. She was twenty-one years old. Marian was four years older. And that was it. For the next twenty-one years, no one knew what had happened.

Then, in 1994, Lucy's remains were discovered in the basement of a flat that had belonged to the serial killers, Fred and Rosemary West. In her memoir, *If You Sit Very Still* – which I cannot recommend too highly – Marian describes the long, complex pathway that led to her finding a response to what happened. It is agonizing to read, and uplifting, and often focuses on the everyday necessity of paying steady, cool attention to whatever is arising in the mind. Rage. Grief. Lethargy. Murderousness. Numbness. Agony. Love. Marian told me that the goal of forgiving the Wests became a goal that helped to orient her through the subsequent years. It seemed impossible, but there was something about that impossibility that made possible all sorts of unexpected developments. Marian's book is a study in the transformations of spiritual intelligence.

She speaks of having to negotiate a process that was going

to be a long haul, though often seemed desperately urgent as her soul sought resolution. Poetry helped her, as did dreams: they provided images, that seemed to come from Lucy and held Marian as she faced the darkness. In time, a very long time, what was a "frozen silence" within her became a "shining silence". I think there's something of the good's commitment to not let us go in that shift.

She also learnt to stay authentic to her experience, and not be led by the drama of events. This was doubly difficult because the media were intensely interested in her story and, given the constraints of the news bulletin – which today would become the limited characters of a tweet – inevitably led to her story being distorted by being packaged up. She calls it "soundbite suffering".

She had to work over not only to what had happened to Lucy but what had happened to her, and all the wounds and traces it had left within her. Feelings of loss, grasping for recognition, delusions of identity. "It is called the 'human condition', this desire for life to be happy and secure, pleasurable, free from pain. It's what we all desire," she writes.[58] The extreme particularity of her story makes it powerfully universal, a thought that emerged when a Chan master told her something seemingly ridiculous or offensive. "Just know that your suffering is relieving the suffering of others," he said. Retreats and silence provided the space in which she could detect how that might be true, in particular because the approach is not a bypass of suffering. Quite the opposite. "Denial is an important part of survival, but as a conclusive position it is an attempt to avoid, trivialize and negate or delay the pain of the healing process, fix it and make it more comfortable to live with," she explains. "Denial can lead to lethal, oppressive regimes... it carries a perverse power which can haunt, oppress and sometimes destroy vitality."[59]

Gradually, the present came back to her, as she attended to what was arising. Its possibilities helped her let go of yearning for a different past and to make a new relationship with life, conscious of all that had happened. "It is that which takes us out of our small self into the larger self of the whole universe, where we realize that who we are is truly interconnected."[60] And then, the Chan master made sense. If her suffering could help others, then maybe it could help Rosemary West as well. From one point of view, that would be a shocking, unforgiveable thought. But now, she could wish well with no expectation of response or reward – what the *Bhagavad Gita* would call living without attachment. She found that higher dimensional space, as did Virginia Woolf, that transformed her perception of everything.

In time, and through appreciating what has occurred in all its difficulty, that vantage offers the possibility of seeing all things in a different way. It's seen by spiritual intelligence. What we have experienced as unforgiveable, or have perpetrated ourselves, is remembered and known fully, and yet revenge or pain or guilt is no longer the main feeling around. Instead, there's stillness and acceptance – an acceptance born not of an ideal or of the will but of an utterly transparent acknowledgement of everything. It's precisely when, and only when, the impossibility of forgiveness is faced, without blinking, that this might break through. Forgiveness is needed because, with the most difficult aspects of life, which are the most important, the best course of action is not to try to fix things but to stay with them, and wait for a radically different horizon to be glimpsed. It is like a death to self and is possible because, at one level, everything is already forgiven, not in secular life or, typically, in human hearts, but in the domain to which we are connected. The good has a commitment to not let us go.

The human heart is like a seed that sprouts and grows into a flower that is too big for the constrained worlds of Ulro, Generation and even Beulah. With the infinite openness of true humility, which is not about self-abnegation or putting yourself last, or not seeking a room of one's own, there can be found a receptivity that can never stop being filled with more.

Dante likens humility to the sea, because the sea's lowest place in nature means that everything can and does flow into it. It can be said to be humble, not because of what it does, but because of how it welcomes, without condition. Similarly, the human person can know all things because they can be open to all things, whether good or the worst evil. This humility is freeing, too, because it is the quality that enables the individual to turn to the side of life that they can't own or claim, which is by far the greater part of life. "Humility is a rare virtue and an unfashionable one and one which is often hard to discern," reflects Iris Murdoch. "Only rarely does one meet someone in whom it positively shines, in whom one apprehends with amazement the absence of the anxious avaricious tentacles of the self."[61] Such a person sees "the pointlessness of virtue and its unique value and the endless extent of its demand," she adds. It's an immense thought but, then, we are capable of immensity.

### A quote
"When a contradiction is impossible to resolve except by a lie, then we know that it is really a door." Simone Weil, *Waiting For God*.

### A practice
Developmental psychologists have examined how young children learn to shape their bodies to the world around them, so as better to interact with it. For example, a youngster carefully molds its hand to a cup to pick up the cup.

Virtues are similar. They are the mind molding itself to the world around, thereby enabling us to make better contact with life and so engage with life more fully. So try taking a moment to contemplate an object in front of you. Imagine loving it, and see what that does to your relationship with it. Then imagine fearing it, and see what that does.

## Step 7

# Befriending Irruptions

Virginia Woolf saw a leaf drop on a London street. Joe Gardner watched a sycamore seed fall. Here's a third stirring of foliage that catalyzed a realization. It happened to C.S. Lewis, precipitating another conversion to a wider form of consciousness.

It happened when he was walking in an Oxford park with his friends J.R.R. Tolkien and Hugo Dyson. They were earnestly discussing myths. Lewis was inclined to believe they are fascinating and beautiful but ultimately worthless, whereas Tolkien insisted they convey crucial, dynamic and otherwise hidden truths. It was an engrossing walk and talk, Lewis later told a friend, that was memorably, momentarily stopped – "interrupted by a rush of wind which came so suddenly on the still, warm evening and sent so many leaves pattering down that we thought it was raining. We all held our breath, the other two appreciating the ecstasy of such a thing."

All three Oxford scholars would have known that, to the vast majority of humans, for the vast majority of our evolutionary history, wind was also experienced as breath and spirit. In many ancient languages, a single word designates what are now regarded as the three isolated phenomena. "Pneuma" is the ancient Greek; "ruach" the ancient Hebrew; "prana" carries comparable connotations in Sanskrit; the Chinese character "chi" can imply breath, spirit and the energy of life, including in association with the weather.

It seems that Tolkien and Dyson spontaneously reverted to the older experience, as can happen in moments when eternity surprises the mind. They read the spiritual presence within the rush of wind as they held their own breath. Lewis sensed it too, but checked his perception of the instant, as the leaves became still again. He resisted the invitation. His spiritual intelligence hesitated. But although the wind dropped, the inner rustling did not. He came to see that what his friends had been saying was right. Myths aren't empty.

Years later, Lewis revisited the moment in a poem. He fully understands its significance now, and welcomes it. His verse captures the discovery that has been my main focus in this book – the breakthrough that arises with a quiet, still, apparently humdrum, but radical recognition. Entitled, "What the Bird Said Early in the Year", it is worth looking up and reading. Lewis describes not letting such eruptions of possibility escape your notice, paying attention as they arrive and not watching them slip back over time's horizon, because if you catch one, something remarkable can happen. Instead of continuing along the path that you had presumed was yours, there's a fork. Rather than staying in the trance of the everyday, there is a moment of surprise and choice. Seize it. Be alive to it. Want it. Opt for it. A doorway into a parallel world, that is also here, stands before you. The moment may turn out to be like stepping into a wardrobe and finding Narnia.

The six steps to engage our spiritual intelligence so far explored have all, in a way, been aimed at this chance. The first step was updating the backstory we tell about the evolution of our species: the standard one, which I think is outdated, simply rules spiritual intelligence out. An account of who we are as individuals matters as well, explored in step two: we are free in ways pioneered by the inward turn of the Axial figures. A description of what that freedom allows us to wake up to is step three: being that is closer to us than we are to ourselves. Then, there is the need for a way of working with what can hinder that conscious alignment: there may be a need to settle the soul if a deeper spirit is to be revealed. The manner in which we approach death becomes central, as we came to in step five: it is pivotal, as death may become the daily birth of more. And when our personal qualities resonate with reality, it is liberating: virtues are powered by grace, as we examined in step six.

The seventh step has a twofold purpose. One is to bring the previous steps together under a single attitude or principle. It's not exhaustive but is a development of this openness to reality, focusing on befriending reality when it meets us. Life throws all sorts of interruptions our way – some major, many small – but what it doesn't insist on is how we respond. Our attention to them is always our responsibility and, as we have been exploring, the quality of the imagination and intelligence we apply in response to events dramatically influences the reality that shows up. There's more to say about that.

Before coming to it though, there is a second, linked element. This is to ask how this transformation of attention can become a way of life not only for us as individuals, but in society at large. That matters because no one is an island and the cultures around us can limit perceptual possibilities, or enlarge them. Society's soul affects personal souls – there is no neat boundary between the various levels of vitality – which is why Plato recognized that the organization of a good city has to mirror the pattern of human flourishing, and the Renaissance humanists focused on improving the character of their rulers, hoping this would benefit the commonwealth. My aim here is not to offer a plan, partly because I am not up to that, but also because the principle I want to suggest actually involves sitting lightly to plans. The issue is really about a certain type of education. Spiritual intelligence senses that tomorrow might not be just more of today with improvements. We can learn to anticipate what we had not previously anticipated, and the ways in which genuine novelty might show up.

Highlighting this transformation of attention is important because of the growing consensus that modern civilization is in trouble. We require richer ways of relating to human and nonhuman others, if we are not permanently to injure ourselves and them. My view is that the sidelining of spiritual intelligence lies at the heart of this crisis. Material obsessions and consumer desires are in the driving seat. The economic policies and technological wizardry that are supposed to satisfy these wants are actually unable to control or contain them. They also obscure what is right in front of our noses – put simply, that there is a spiritual commons. It is there for us to know, love, draw from and return to. The question is how, now, culturally and societally, to reconnect with this source.

## The nature of imprisonment

The key factor is that it will require a breakthrough, not as one required when advancing towards well-articulated goals like building a fusion reactor or starting a colony on Mars, but rather as the word originally meant: the penetration of a barrier that has held back sight of another realm entirely. This type of breakthrough is more akin to a rebirth than the elimination of a problem, an experience of astonishment rather than a march of progress, a deepening of communion rather than an extension of power.

It has to be a spiritual breakthrough because the disconnected, modern imagination has, for the most part, turned the cosmos into a vast gallery of intriguing but empty idols. When, culturally speaking, we attend to the universe, we are inclined to see a mix of chaotic and orderly objects. Our awareness has lost sight of the living ecology of celestial and terrestrial images that spoke to our ancestors as readily as thoughts flood into our heads. Instead, we acknowledge our precious spark of sentience, though some scientists tell us even that is dead, and wonder if we are alone, surrounded by entities from planets to plants that barge through the environment like zombies. "That is why we feel detached, isolated, cut off not only from the world as it really is, but also from those other little sparks of detached self-consciousness we acknowledge in our fellow human beings," writes Owen Barfield, another friend of Lewis, whom both Lewis and Tolkien testified to producing the most revolutionary ideas of the three of them.[62]

Life has become a type of imprisonment, which some know because of pervasive unease or mental ill-health, and others show by rioting in cities or fleeing to hoped-for utopias. The prison walls are not built of concrete – which would be better because we could see them to take down – but mental habits, which are far more insidious. They are repaired and reinforced almost every time an authority in the sciences, literature, the arts, psychology, sociology or politics speaks – and, not infrequently, when authorities in religion speak too. Don't listen to what these people say, listen to the metaphors they use. "Reboots", "upgrades", "coding", "reprogramming", "hacking", "adapting", "optimizing". They are metaphors of the mechanical mind. They almost overwhelmingly shape the public conversation and won't bring life because, inadvertently or not, the language of the discussion is quietly closing life down. "It is not just my mental habit, or your mental habit. It is *our* mental habit," Barfield continues. "I can philosophize myself free from philosophical materialism quite easily; and so, I dare say, can you. But what we are talking about is *collective* mental habit, which is a very different matter." Nihilism, naturalism, postmodernism, the detached rationalism that regards itself as self-evident common sense. Call it what you will. It shapes our thoughts and structures our perceptions. There is no pneuma, it insists. There is wind and there is breath and there is possibly spirit – if that is understood as a metaphor for frivolous, momentary chutzpah. "As long as we have done nothing to change this common sense, this subconscious foundation of our consciousness, we have not begun the business of escaping at all," Barfield asserts.

In a world enclosed by a materialist imagination, reentering the spiritual commons requires doing what the ideology tells you can't be done. It's a big task, but can begin immediately, in every moment, with actually a modest step. The key begins to turn when we actively pay attention to the meaning of what happens. Don't keep eyes ahead: look up or down. Don't hold your breath: take it in. Materialism's praetorian guard, which you have more or less certainly introjected simply by virtue of living in the twenty-first century, will instantly raise its pikes. It will issue threats, stares and mockery that can be more effective than the best equipped surveillance state – but what the guard don't want you to know is it can be disarmed in an instant. When the leaves rustle, pause. When the sycamore seed drops, look. There is, in fact, nothing stopping you. This is the inner freedom, gained in the Axial period, that cannot be bound.

## *The reopening of the cosmos*

In truth, there are some in authority challenging the guard too. It's increasingly common to hear smart, informed individuals wondering whether they must think obliquely. Others may be having a quiet conversation in their heads. "Could the light of intelligence and love, which I know in myself, belong to a radiance that shines from a complex and ultimately undivided whole? It does seem odd that only humans have it. Plus, there's that online meditation app. It tells me to watch 'the breath'. Why 'the breath'? Might it do something to me? 'Treat the breath as a vitality flowing within and without,' it said. 'Consider whether it might be a sustaining lifeforce or spirit, just for a while.' I did feel a bit calmer and connected."

The officially sanctioned, Möbius strip model of reality, which loops back on itself, is perhaps coming undone. The closed system could be opening up. We've already considered some of the ways – revising humanity's evolutionary backstory, considering history's interiority and the soul within science, taking virtues and values as guides to reality. But the broader point is that the modern assumption is precisely that: an assumption that has become an ingrained habit. And it can be shown to be inadequate. Take a simple example. We all intuit truths, as opposed to empirically proving and testing them. You learn them from your earliest days at school. 1+1=2. Some of the intuitions of geniuses have proven hugely fruitful when developed. They are like rain from above, falling on the sciences and the arts, which soon shrivel without them. So where do these intuitions come from, upon which the cosmos appears to rest?

The reflections of scientists not bound by anti-religious reflexes have developed the question. The physicist, John Polkinghorne, who was part of the team that derived the existence of quarks, was one. He used to talk about the "open grain" of the universe. He wondered whether information might ray its influence through this porous texture, remaining hidden because what can't be explained by mechanistic forms of causality is, within the closed world of scientific materialism, dismissed as chance. Chance, after all, is supposed to be the reason the cosmos is right for life – and, even more remarkably, to be intelligible to at least some of the minds it has nurtured. But the products of this presumed randomness appear remarkably unchance-like to many when you look. That's led another physicist, Paul Davies, to propose a "life principle" that draws the universe towards life, consciousness and qualities like love, much like riverbanks guide water to the sea. Riverbanks are formed as well as discovered, and can erode and fail, though when they do, they are soon remade, and the flow picks up again, in more or less the same direction. So, too, with the universe, it seems.

Alternatively, there are those who have noticed that whilst the sciences have tremendous powers of explanation within specified domains, it is an act of faith that assumes they are all linked together. Understanding bosons will tell you nothing about baboons. Even within single sciences, there exist vast inconsistencies. An obvious example is the incompatibility of general relativity, which is hugely successful at describing things on a large scale, and quantum theory, which is astonishingly successful at the small scale. But one insists the universe is determined, the other insists it is not. The philosopher of science, Nancy Cartwright, asks whether the patchiness of science is because, at a physical level, the universe is dappled. This does not mean that it is full of sockets and holes, into which an interventionist demiurge can insert screwdrivers and spanners for occasional adjustments and tweaks, as Intelligent Design supposes. The dappling is more like the sunlight in a forest, as beams and rays refract through waving leaves on trees. In this analogy, the sun is the origin, the source of reality and the spiritual commons, which can be intuitively known but not empirically captured. Science stands on the floor of the forest, as it were, examining the light scattered by the canopy overhead. It is unsurpassed at studying isolated spots. But equally fascinating to ask is how the dots join up.

Such questions are prompting discussions of possibilities that were beyond the pale when I was an undergraduate physicist, including the merits of panpsychism, the need for an extended evolutionary synthesis in biology that abandons the selfish gene, participative models of cognition in which sentience co-creates reality, and emergent models in cosmology. They will be interesting to watch and, I hope, will be culturally significant so as to help expand the collective imagination. Although, there is no need to wait. Do you see the guinea-sun or the heavenly host crying "Holy! Holy! Holy!"? That can be worked on right now. It may even help spread new science.

What we need is a taste for the seemingly extraordinary that spiritual intelligence brings. There is a way of developing that taste that can become a social as well as personal experience. This is the principle I want to suggest. It is an attitude that can bring about a renewal of meaning by focusing on interrupting the usual experience of time.

## *Introducing kairos*

Our times are, importantly, called secular. The word originally comes from the Latin, saeculum, meaning an epoch or era, though it came to be used as one term in an opposition. That happened first in church circles, to distinguish between religious clergy who followed the pattern of the day set by the monastic liturgy of the hours, and secular clergy, for whom this-worldly concerns could intervene. The two ways of organizing the day then moved into political theory, so that nowadays, secular people are embedded in a type of time that is shaped not by rituals but the clock. A secular world is oriented around the timepiece. It keeps the trains running and, in a capitalist society, monetizes the day by commoditizing time that is invested, wasted or lost. A secular world simultaneously tends to turn from other ways of experiencing time, especially the type called eternity, which may well be dismissed, along with concepts like the spiritual.

Defying secular time's monopoly is my suggested strategy, because there are plenty of alternatives. There is the kind often associated with Plato, in which time is viewed as the "moving image of eternity". Or there is cyclical time, within which the cosmos returns to an original state across a period measured by the great years, traversed by the stars. Another variant has been called the "time of origins", by the historian of religion, Mircea Eliade. This is an ever-present, celebrated moment – perhaps mythical, perhaps historic – that is invoked as a source of identity and energy in folk traditions, often associated with place. A further expression of time developed after the Axial period. It is the experience of time that strongly differentiates between past, present and future, so that the past is taken to resource or lead up to the present, which in turn contains a projection of the future. The present is a moment that the secular worldview came to experience as the growing tip of progress, although the original Axial perception was different. It attended to the potential inherent in the present that can break through and revolutionize the moment. The Axial figures are cases in point, individuals whose short lives were experienced as axes around which, longer-term, civilizations altered and changed. They didn't have plans. They didn't champion progress. They did live a new sense of time and it changed everything.

It is a type of time sometimes called apocalyptic, from the Greek for uncovering, and sometimes messianic time, which emerged after Saint Paul realized that the Second Coming of Jesus wasn't to be expected at some future date, but was instead to be known in the here and now. It led him to wrestle with what it means to be "in the world but not of the world". It also differentiated what became mainstream Christianity from millenarianism, in which the moment of disruption is not anticipated as an inner reorientation or conversion, but as a climactic event that will overturn time and whisk away the chosen.

My principle is the Axial idea of apocalyptic time, though renamed, to make it less ominous and more immediate. This is important because, much as I've been demythologizing spectacular accounts of the awakening called enlightenment, so I want to show how the irruptions in the present that can reorientate us are quietly happening all the time. We just need the eyes to see and ears to hear them. The word I have in mind is kairos, after the Greek meaning the right or opportune time. It's the sense of time used in expressions like "a great comic has good timing" or "it's time to change". It understands that whatever is needed is available and can be utilized now, and so attending to what's happening now, as opposed to being preoccupied with the future or the past, is its approach.

Kairos contrasts with clock time, which was called chronos. It is used as a means of measurement, not quality, to describe the steady, sequential progress of weeks and days, as opposed to the kairos attention that spots the timeliness of a particular insight or instant. Early uses of kairos are illuminating. It could describe the precise moment to pass a shuttle cleanly through a loom when weaving quality cloth. Penelope, in the *Odyssey*, was said to be a wily practitioner of this kairos art. When she was waiting for the return of Odysseus, she used it to keep herself free, famously outwitting her suitors with her weaving by day and unweaving by night. It was also used in the ancient study of rhetoric, describing the ability of an orator to deliver a line with perfect timing so as to transform the mood of an audience. Boom.

When we're attending to the world in kairos time, and the world is manifesting itself to us similarly, we experience people and places as present, vivid, distinctive and here. Conversely, when we're attending to the world in chronos time, and the world is manifesting itself in the same way, we experience people and places as existing, executing, objective, and there. Kairos time means we can attend to what's happening and receive its value, whereas chronos time treats everything that happens equally, as another event that merely arrives and passes by. It's why W.H. Auden's famous poem about death, which is not just another event, demanded that the clocks be stopped. It is an offence that they keep nonchalantly ticking.

In kairos, we live time. In chronos, we live in time. Kairos cuts, chronos chugs. The classification of a state of mind described as boredom first appears in the eighteenth century, about the same time as secular chronos attained its near monopoly. It made us "passive recipients," suggests Iain McGilchrist, in his great book, *The Master and His Emissary*.[63] Kairos time is not like that. It might be marked by terror, confusion, melancholy or paralysis, but never boredom.

There is an equivalent of the rabbit-duck illusion that can be played to feel the difference between kairos and chronos. For instance, if I say that the batsman struck the ball which flew off in a particular direction, that would be describing the incident in chronos time, from the vantage of an onlooker or observer. But if I say that the ball flew off in a particular direction because the batsman struck it in a certain way, that would be more in kairos. The perspective of the batsman is being drawn attention to, as an active agent in the moment the bat strikes the ball. He or she wanted the ball to fly to the boundary or, perhaps, to the offside, and so designed an impact to bring it about. Kairos, similarly, knows that moments are shaped by agency, rather than being meaningless or blind.

Alternatively, imagine a swimmer getting into trouble in the water and being thrown a rubber ring by a passerby. It turns out that the swimmer is religious and had prayed for help just before the passerby approached. A moment of distress became loaded with significance: kairos. However, the passerby is thoroughly secular-minded and so, when afterwards, the swimmer exclaims, "You are an answer to prayer!", the passerby thinks: no, I just happened to be there. Chronos. One person's chance incident is another's telling synchronicity.

Or again, consider once more that everyday intuition, 1+1=2. Socrates told of an occasion when, one day, it was raining in Athens. He watched the shower and happened to see two raindrops collide. They came close, touched, merged. And he asked himself: have I observed something completely ordinary or an astonishing minor miracle? The chronos habit unthinkingly opts for the former: raindrop coalescence is the process by which raindrops form and grow, it might explain later, which is true. But the kairos mentality knows something else. What had been two became one. What had been dual and divided became singular and united. So where did the quality of twoness go and where did the quality of oneness come from? Socrates was gripped because he felt he had been shown a process that doesn't just form raindrops but operates at the deepest levels of the cosmos. There was magic in the sight, not merely the working of a mechanism.

## Birthdays and big histories
Human beings need kairos time to enliven chronos, which is

why manifestations of it keep appearing. Take the marking of cycles, like birthdays and the New Year. They commemorate the passing of chronos time but are simultaneously occasions when it seems auspicious to take stock or make resolutions, in the hope the agency of the moment might be seized, for a break into a different future. Similarly, significant birthdays can precipitate unwanted kairos time, such as when a person feels they are passing into old age or entering a midlife crisis.

A less deniable irruption is the moment expectant parents welcome their child. Freud noted how parents completely rearrange their lives for the arrival, to whom he gave an appropriate title: His or Her Majesty the Baby. Like the presence of royalty, a baby absorbs all the attention, partly for practical reasons, partly because their arrival is so extraordinary, and yet at the same time unexceptional. That combination of wonderful and normal is the sign of an oblique, kairos irruption. It can be nightmarish. "Since you arrived, days have melted into night and back again and we are learning a new grammar, a long sentence whose punctuation marks are feeding and winding and nappy changing and these occasional moments of quiet," explained Fergal Keane in his tender, *Letter to Daniel*. But even when it's nightmarish, there are cracks in the haze of days merging with nights, when the world lights up. "You can't understand it until you experience the simple joy of the first time your son points at a seagull and says 'duck'," remarked Russell Crowe.

I wonder if the modern interest in history is driven by a desire to differentiate time, particularly because certain periods of history grab the attention much more than others: it is not history itself that is of interest but the history that has kairos power. Hence, in the UK, books on the Tudors or the Second World War always top the best-seller lists. They promise to awaken, for Brits, what is a time of origins. Relatedly, the appeal of big history is the quest for an overarching narrative to make sense of it all. Narration is a way of adding texture to chronos time and can also be used to derail chug-time's dominance.

A kairos appreciation of time is similarly encouraged by references to equinoxes and solstices, or by the juxtaposition of the Gregorian calendar with Hijri or lunisolar calendars. The effect is to reconnect to cycles and seasons. The cultural critic, Walter Benjamin, called it a resistance to "homogeneous, empty time". He suggested that bold historians mightn't tell of events as a sequence of social and political causes and effect, but as constellations of themes and occurrences, with links and resonances that reach across time. The present could be reframed as "shot through with splinters of messianic time," he wrote, exploring how it is shaped by a blend of kairos and chronos. Such a history would be akin to Plutarch's *Parallel Lives*, in which the Roman historian presented biographies in pairs to draw attention to timeless virtues and vices. Reflecting on the family resemblance of Axial figures from around the globe is a similar undertaking, showing how periods have a spirit as well as a date.

The popularity of festivals is another moment when we encounter what Charles Taylor calls "kairotic knots".[64] Gathering in a country field or landscaped park, away from creature comforts and familiar surroundings often colored by work, is a way of recalling medieval carnivals, when the world is turned upside down. This used to involve making children into bishops, subjecting kings to ordeals, and turning supposed fools into leaders, and today festivals still mock the regulation and ordering of peoples and events with celebrations of ecstatic music and arresting ideas, or an indulgence of drugs, chaos and laughter akin to a Saturnalia. Other festivals may provide an opportunity for rededication, especially those that have a religious theme, or again may remind people of solidarity, excitement and excellence, such as can be experienced at the Olympics.

Another kairotic knot that regularly shows up in the modern world is in relation to care. In one way, we live in an era of unparalleled care, in the form of the welfare state and advanced medicine, at least in the places that can afford it. What is striking, though, is how moved the cared for are by any personal touches received during treatment. Once recovered, former patients often make extravagant and entirely genuinely claims about the care they have received, such as that they have never been better cared for than by their nurses. The emotional excess behind the thanks comes, I think, because it is not just that they have been treated by an efficient and effective system, but they have felt the humanity of a kairos encounter too. They felt they were treated as a person, in the context of relationship, in spite of the bureaucracy. Love was unexpectedly present. For Ivan Illich, this was the significance of the parable of the Good Samaritan. It teaches precisely the opposite of the requirement to offer care, by focusing on the free spontaneity of the good Samaritan's attention to the beaten-up Jew. He saw a person, not an abstract need.

## *Touching eternity*

Kairos experiences can be used not to overwrite chronos, but to bring the two types of time together. Music's power partly derives from its ability to do this and, to make the point, consider the contrast with muzak. The latter will be produced by an artificial intelligence, working solely within chronos time, as its microprocessors execute a trillion tidy instructions per second to produce the tune that it fails to comprehend. But an unwitting listener will immediately get it as their spiritual intelligence automatically kicks in and puts chronos and kairos together. They will be affected by it, which is of course the point – be that to feel lulled or stimulated or irritated.

That process is very different from an intentional music audience, which is out to experience a deliberately composed intersection of time and eternity. The literary critic, George Steiner, argued this is why live music has become an essential experience, as it liberates us "from the enforcing beat of biological and physical-mathematical clocks. The time which music 'takes', and which it gives as we perform or experience it, is the only free time granted us prior to death," he wrote.[65] I don't think it's the only free time before death. But Steiner's hyperbole makes a point, and again underlines why music is so widely used for relating to the spiritual commons, all the way back to the earliest days of Homo sapiens and, most likely, long before and by other species. Great music stirs the latency of eternity.

William Blake was clear that kairos is crucial. It connects us to eternity, not meant as the indefinite prolongation of time, but rather as the meaning of existence in the here and now. "Eternity Exists, and All Things in Eternity," he firmly concluded.

It needn't be an exceptional experience that reveals this, though. One way to know it comes when someone feels that they have acted as their best selves or, perhaps less commonly, when they find themselves doing something more admirable than they thought they were capable of. The afterglow of a deed well done spreads through them like a flame, because to act well is to act truly, and truth is eternal, Blake explained. Choosing to behave in ways that are true, beautiful or good is consciously to align your being with our origins, in eternity. We're in it anyway, the poet continued, but it is invigorating to attend to and know, even if the price of doing so is costly. It's another reflection of self-sacrifice, and why people will go to the extent of dying for others and ideas. They are asserting that they are not "a worm of sixty winters" but dwell in "the divine body", to use Blakean expressions that neatly distinguish chronos and kairos.

Conversely, the presence of eternity in time explains why being dishonest or manipulative feels degrading, even if no one else knows about it. The sense of shame or pollution is a more or less conscious awareness that you have turned your back on your rightful home. "A truth that's told with bad intent, Beats all the lies you can invent," Blake wrote in *Auguries of Innocence*, a collection of aphorisms that can be read as designed to reawaken kairos.

The prophet understands kairos, Blake continued. They are not individuals who attend to cards or the stars in an effort to predict the future, but rather are the conveyors of the tremendous significance of the present – which is why the best artists are prophets. The characters created by Dickens or Shakespeare are timeless because their personalities and actions express matters of weight or precariousness that transcend times and places, though they are totally rooted in them too. There's that joining of the particular and the universal again. To watch a play is to see characters immersed in moments when chronos time grows thin and kairos time erupts with tragedy or comedy, romance or catharsis.

The great artists of nature similarly reveal the world's kairos qualities. Such works close our "vegetative eyes", which are inclined to focus on nature's transience or treat time as a record, and open up "Visions of Eternity". Blake's own art aspires to do this, which is why he shows angels in sunsets, daemons in stars, deities in flowers, and beasts within vines. It is art designed to reveal the omnipresent vitality in animate organisms and inanimate forms. Seeing a Van Gogh cornfield or pair of boots means that such things need never look the same again: they have been revealed as they truly are. It's why a Barbara Hepworth sculpture, of graceful and bold, monumental and gently confusing shapes, feels intensely poetic and as if you are seeing the familiar afresh, for the very first time. It's why David Hockney's bright paintings of *The Arrival of Spring in Normandy* prompt involuntary gasps of joy. When you delight in his greens and yellows you don't only see fields and trees but also the buzzing, in between spaces – the eternity out of which the fields and trees spring, Blake might say. "This world of Imagination is the world of Eternity; it is the divine bosom into which we shall go after the death of the Vegetated body."

Not that Blake is against the transient world, at all. He was sure nothing of it would be lost. But he wants us to see it as the unveiling of eternity, so that the everyday might be transformed.

## The spiritually intelligent body

Explicitly religious and spiritual practices are a further crucial way in which kairos time is accessed – and I stress practices rather than beliefs. They matter too, but I think that part of the reason the Western world, at least, is losing touch with this key way of charting alternative tomorrows erupting today is because of the modern stress on beliefs, rather than activities. What gets lost is the power of the body to expand our ways of knowing. In his book, *A Plea For Embodied Spirituality*, the psychologist, Fraser Watts, unpacks the way it works.

He takes as an example the elaborate rituals traditionally demanded of worshippers at a Siva temple. The follower must inhabit certain virtues, described as Siva's limbs, which are cultivated by control of the body, exercised through requirements like not eating meat or drinking alcohol. Attire matters, including wearing ash and beads called "the eyes of Rudra", as does ritual washing, prostrations and circumambulations that are embodied marks of respect for the deity, and a way of welcoming divine power. During particular pujas, the temple must be regularly attended because it is a symbolic womb, embracing an inner sanctum containing the lingam. An offering of food or flowers completes the acknowledgement of a potent spiritual exchange.

The body matters in all this because bodies can only be in the present moment and so, when attended to, can be utilized to increase the chances of a kairos experience, facilitating receipt of a word or blessing from the god. They create an openness to liminality, which Watts notes is amplified by other features of a temple, such as the contrast between the movement of the devotees and the stillness of the statues. "Verticality among worshippers performing puja, with its control of the body as means to holiness, is in contrast with the rhythmic, asymmetrical and transversal poses of statues of deities adorning thousands of temples. An outsider to the faith may see this contrast as a disjunction, but a larger, unspoken gestalt may be at work," Watts writes. The deities' abundance, expressed in their lithe beauty, is available to the devotee, who shows readiness in ritual and movement. What the gods live and love gracefully, the follower can aspire physically to know. The body is a vehicle for direct communion.

Pascal was right: "If you perform religious rites with enthusiasm... you will come to be devoutly religious," the philosopher wrote. The conclusion is sneered at by rationalists, who will put any surge of belief down to neediness or delusion, though ironically this attitude is itself a religious one. It originates with the way ritual and the body came to be frowned upon by a certain type of believer, at the time of the Reformation. This was a moment when a presumed gulf between the divine and mere mortals was stressed. Human fallenness was the preoccupation of figures like Martin Luther and John Calvin. They taught that it needs to be overcome by being confessed and acknowledged. As a result, the body became suspect, with rituals being declared blasphemous and pagan, because they seemed to imply a denial of the presumed gulf. Divine communion couldn't possibly be as easy as lighting a candle or bowing to a saint. The objections are worth noting because they inadvertently underline the extraordinary capacity of the body to access the spiritual kairotically.

Just how that works is explored in what is called embodied cognition, which the psychologist, James Jones, examines in his book, *Living Religion: Embodiment, Theology, and the Possibility of Spiritual Sense*. Jones summarizes recent findings in the field. For example, if individuals look down when trying to remember something, their powers of recall are boosted. Alternatively, memory improves when associated with places, which is why recollections come flooding back when you visit an old haunt or home. There's good evidence that a sluggish body posture amplifies depressed feelings and sitting up or standing straight gives a boost to self-esteem. Going for a walk enhances discernment, with the implication that going on a pilgrimage to work out what you believe is very sensible. Another experiment that shows the link between motion and mentation can be done at home. Try explaining something to a friend whilst keeping your arms by your sides. When you can't gesticulate, it is very much harder. Gestures are bodily correlates of thoughts, as well as actions that help us think. They are not an optional extra.

Iain McGilchrist highlights another reason for focusing on the body when building spiritual intelligence. In his work on brain lateralization, the psychiatrist and philosopher explains how the left hemisphere's narrower focus supports the capacity to control the world, whereas the right hemisphere sustains the capacity to maintain an open, uncertain engagement. If the left longs to make the world its own, the right receives. If the left conceptualizes, the right is expectant. The two are in a creative tension in a way that parallels chronos and kairos. The point is not that the right hemisphere is spiritual, and the left the source of secular inclinations. The truth is that the most valuable spiritual insights live where the two worldviews meet.

That said, there will be reduced spiritual intelligence if the perceptions of the right hemisphere are disabled or dismissed. McGilchrist stresses that this is why a meaning crisis pervades our times and we feel imprisoned. We have been overwhelmed by the offspring of chronos in the form of bureaucratic, progressive, common sensical, manualized, behavioral, self-referential, epicycle-like, treadmill-like, procedural, monocultural, monetized ways of organizing our lives. There's a reason why the old deity called Chronos was thought to eat his children. Many feel as if they are being consumed by linear time now.

McGilchrist adds that any remedying of the situation will stress the importance of the body because the right hemisphere is more deeply connected to it. Both hemispheres have motor and sensory connections with the body. But whereas the left makes maps, the right carries a whole-body sense that is intimately linked to lived, affective experience. It is responsible for empathic connections with others and the world and, we might surmise, the awareness of kairos. It brings expansive feeling and spiritual intuition.

On occasion, that can make bodily actions appear nothing short of magical. For instance, if you imagine doing something, it's more likely that you'll be able to do it. A person who visualizes lifting a heavy weight stands a better chance of being able to lift it. "Thought is a whole-body activity," James Jones stresses. Singing, dancing, standing and sitting; breathing, visualizing, bowing and hand-raising; sacred places, holy spaces, pilgrimage sites and special seasons. They work with the connection between mind and body. Such rituals do not just support belief, they deepen real perceptions. "Reverence is not simply a virtue for which we may expect full marks in heaven," wrote Owen Barfield. "It is an organ of perception for a whole range of qualities that are imperceptible without it."[66] If our times are to regain this range of seemingly imperceptible qualities, the body's knowing, along with this assortment of activities, will be central.

## Science and the meaning crisis
This could include science, in that a recovery and appreciation of kairos might assist future shifts in physics and philosophy. It's a speculative suggestion, though not my own. The physicist, David Bohm, made the link with his recognition that "knowledge tends to get caught in grooves and compartments which become rather rigid," as he observed in a symposium and conversation with Owen Barfield.[67] "Insight is what dissolves

these grooves and compartments and opens the way for reason and imagination to engage in fresh perception," he continued.

The link between insights and the nature of time fascinated him. Consider this conundrum. If the present is the point between the past that no longer exists and the future that doesn't yet exist, the implication is that the present is the join between periods of duration that don't exist. To put it another way, if you consider time to be a concrete actuality, it collapses, which is why it might be better to think of it as a map. In its chronos form, it orders the territory of reality, perhaps by tidily relating events or, alternatively, by systematically arranging thoughts. That can be valuable, but time isn't just chronos.

Kairos time would work differently, as illuminated by pondering the etymological link between moment and movement. Bohm was attracted to these words' shared root, located in the Latin word, momentum, meaning "moving power". It powerfully resonated with his theory that the tangible world, which he called the explicate order, is an unfolding of an intangible parallel world, which he called the implicate order. Moments in time, be they measured in fractions of second, as an atomic physicist might, or in centuries and years, as a historian might, can be understood as the movement from the implicate to the explicate order. Understood in this way, moments are not chronos-like, as if they follow as equal units one after the other, but are kairos-like, as they erupt with different qualities into the present. There would be a counter movement as well, in which a moment in the present was introjected from the explicate back into the implicate order. It would be experienced as a significant moment in time.

It's an interesting way of reflecting on the role of time in relation to the advance of knowledge, and why the intuitions of kairos are so significant. Bohm's sense is that insights unfold from the implicate order to disturb the rigid grooves of current knowledge and offer fresh perceptions.

Albert Einstein would have put it differently, by focusing on the human imagination, but in terms of the dynamic, he agreed. He had a strong conviction we are given imagination, in part, so that reality might be unveiled to us. That happens by paying attention to the qualities it loves, such as simplicity and beauty. For this reason, Einstein thought the scientist and the poet essentially work in the same way. "It is a sudden illumination, almost a rapture. Later, to be sure, intelligence analyses and experiments confirm or invalidate the intuition. But initially there is a great leap forward of the imagination," he said.[68] There is a moment of kairos, which happens because of what Bohm called "the non-straightness of thought". Little wonder, Alfred North Whitehead, another giant of philosophy and early twentieth century science, called kairos the time of "creative advance."

Who knows: maybe the universe itself operates with a mix of chronos and kairos time? That might be expected, given that human intelligence resonates with cosmic intelligibility, which could happen only if they mirror each other in important ways. If the human mind can leap forward, maybe the universe can too – and there might be test cases. I'm thinking of what is called strong emergence and whether it could be thought of as a manifestation of cosmic kairos. Weak emergence happens when a new thing appears that makes sense in relation to what has existed before. Strong emergence happens when a new thing appears that does not make sense in relation to what has existed before. The emergence of life is an example because, whilst there are many theories about the conditions required for the emergence of life, no one has any idea how it actually happened. It looks to be a cosmic leap forward, and therefore perhaps happens in kairos time. That's sheer speculation on my part, but maybe even imaginatively thinking in that way might assist in the development of a properly robust scientific theory.

## *Open uncertainty*

Kairos is important in another form of non-straight questing, dialogues. The point about a true dialogue is not that two people talk, but that their exchange is designed to be open to an intuition or insight that neither party, of themselves, could have had. A dialogue does not just proceed in chronos time, as one person makes a contribution, followed by the other, like a dreary radio interview. It needs to include a sense of kairos time as well, for the moments when both speakers feel the "a-ha" of a realization that emerges from between or beyond them.

It was built into older dialogical practices. Plato knits two key qualities into his Socratic dialogues that foster it. One is aporia, or impasse. These moments come during and at the end of the exchange, after much has been said, showing that there is still more to be discovered, which it is not yet possible to articulate. The aporia create a sense of pregnant wonder, as if awaiting on a kairotic intervention.

The second quality is friendship. When a dialogue goes well, goodwill builds between those dialoguing. The amity deepens as they take risks with what they say, correlating with the extent to which they open up to one another. That, in turn, supports the openness that makes for realization, partly because it creates an atmosphere of undefended welcome; partly because the domain of uncertainty from which kairotic revelations come is increasingly recognized as worth befriending. The dialogical art is to give what you have and be inquiring of more, as opposed to being dismissive of the unknown or frustrated with it.

A parallel practice is found in Tibetan Buddhism. The Brahmodya is a ritualized and competitive dialogue, with the aim of expressing truths beautifully, until the competitors can say no more. When they fail to speak further, the speakers fall into a silence that captures the ineffable. Such practices may be useful for all sorts of reasons, but one in particular is relevant to spiritual intelligence. It can make a space for that which exists but can't be spoken.

It is called ineffability and comes after everything that might be said has been volunteered. The silence can then point to the unknown more. It is a sacred moment because it stands for what isn't grasped, but is intuitively known. These truths exist at the "edge of words", as the theologian, Rowan Williams, has described it. They are in a realm in which knowledge and ignorance couple, and are appreciated by the transcendent virtue of intellectual humility.

Science honors this mode of understanding when questions are answered by better questions. It matters when thinking about the spiritual commons, whose boundless qualities are well expressed by paradoxes that point to the ineffable. Its eternity includes time. Its life includes death. Its freedom rests on GCtNLUG, though to be meaningful that freedom must include the possibility of tragedy. It enwombs all things but is also enwombed by things that have soul. Its transcendence is beyond all things, which also means it is completely free to be immanent within everything. Its movement is rest, not restlessness, as Dante realizes in the complete satisfaction he experiences when spinning perfectly with "the love that moves the sun and the other stars". Its unity is a diversity, rather than an undifferentiated uniformity, because a diverse unity is richer than a singularity, much as the unity of an orchestra is richer than single instruments, though they can each play solos too.

Intellectual reverence in the form of the ineffable is an organ of perception. You can sense its validity by seeing how the aim of aporia is to include all that we need to be human, and not simply drop them because they can't be expressed. Conversely, a poor form of the ineffable labels something unspeakable in an attempt to exclude it. Consciousness, for those who call it an illusion, would be an example. It then hangs around in a shadowy zone of half-knowledge, perhaps behind a curtain marked "The Hard Problem".

## *Therapy and education*

Psychotherapy is another practice familiar with the value of full silence. It similarly draws on kairos, which is one of the things that differentiates it from more behavioral approaches to the treatment of mental ill-health. The latter depend on evidence which implies that if this is done, that effect will likely follow. Keep a gratitude diary and you may become gladder of life. Tidy your bedroom and you may discover the equanimity that comes with taking responsibility. But psychotherapy says, let's not rush to fix this, if you can bear it, because such solutionism may miss the truly transformative point. Reckoning with yourself in a crisis can be a tropological turning point followed by a realization, with the therapy being the container or space to receive and develop the insight. The confusion and – when it is not overwhelming – the suffering can bring awareness of possibilities not previously considered. A breakdown may be the downside of a breakthrough, the descent before an ascent.

There is a story Teresa of Ávila told about a mishap she had on a journey which illustrates the point. Crossing a small river, she fell into the icy water. Realizing the dousing could be fatal, she called out to God: "Lord, how can you permit such things!" Then she laughed. She realized that her cry was because the incident brought a felt experience of a divine power she didn't understand. The ominous can prompt the numinous. It may also prompt personal development if, instead of a yell and complaint, there is a moment of pause and lingering, in which the individual choses not simply to react in rage, or retreat, but absorb and try to make something of the situation from resources within themselves. Tolerating the tension can call forth a response that inquires of the numinous and so draws closer to it. It's an advantage often won in silence, and lost in self-justifying talk.

Jung was particularly alert to the experience of being surrounded by such irrational kairos, and the expansion of consciousness it can bring. When treating people, he would wait rather than haste to make things better. It is an art, learnt only with experience and, of course, open to abuse. But he wrote: "If I am faced with this problem in analysis I may say: 'Well, let's wait and see what the dreams turn up, or whether higher powers will intervene, perhaps through illness or death. In any case don't decide now. You and I are not God.'" The therapist's confession of not knowing has a healing effect. The patient feels themselves to have been taken seriously. They have not been treated as a thing to be fixed but a soul to be understood. The loneliness and isolation of much suffering has been bridged, as the two wait in the moment, trusting the spiritual commons.

There are huge implications in this for mental health, and further ones for education too because, as the philosopher, Simone Weil, argued, studying is, at base, similar. It is about developing parallel qualities of attention. It is about lessening reliance on a wrestling attention, which believes struggle and effort produce results, and increasing awareness of a contemplative attention, led by beauty and desire, which waits on the matter in hand as it opens up.

Although she doesn't put it this way herself, the distinction maps onto the difference between chronos and kairos. A student caught up in chronos will presume that the quantity of time they put into studying is what counts, an attitude nowadays amplified by the centralized control of curricula that dictate, hour by hour, what the teacher must instruct. But a student who understands kairos will know when to stop and start, as will their teacher. "Twenty minutes of concentrated, untired attention is infinitely better than three hours of the kind of frowning application that leads us to say with a sense of duty done: 'I have worked well!'" Weil writes.[69] The twenty minutes was kairos time, and developing a taste for it is better than the reading of many books. It understands that patience is part of learning because the most precious gifts are obtained by paying attention to what the moment brings, not by disciplining the mind to reach a destination or goal. Love and joy are what sustain the process, not anxiety and sweat.

All these things make sense to spiritual intelligence, which is to say that thinking through the delivery of mental health services and education is an opportunity not just to improve them, but is an opportunity to restore a lost awareness of the world. An education that is not learning by rote, or cramming so as to pass exams, will introduce the student to kairos as well as chronos, and bring that back into society. It would be a form of bildung, to use the word that captures education in the sense of being personally formed, rather than just produced, so as to be able to author oneself and offer something regenerative back to society. There is nothing more important that a society does than educate its children, and it can do so in this rich sense. It could prevent them from being eaten by Chronos.

## Ecological expansions

Such an education might assist the embrace of ecological damage as well, by strengthening people as they learn about what is going on in the natural world. This is an enormously complex subject, of course. The climate crisis will require personal habits and societies as a whole to change. This is to say that it demands of us a conversion, which might be supported, in part, by cultivating kairos. My sense is that it will be a crucial complement when issuing moral demands that people change their behavior because, on its own, such requirements weigh people down with hopeless guilt, and imply the enjoyment of life must shrink. Kairos can make a difference. It is an invitation to step into another relationship with the world that is richer and an enlargement.

More thoughts from Anthony Ashley Cooper help, particularly as they were taken up by Goethe. The German polymath realized that to behold nature in a living way means following her ways. "It is up to us to adapt ourselves to what the phenomena have to show – and not primarily to adapt them to our habitual ways of knowing," he wrote.[70] This responsiveness is appealing because, in nature, there are many forms of existence and varieties of living that can fascinate and delight the soul. The enjoyment of the natural world is not just about entertainment or distraction but can become part of our growth: nature's diversity invites us to know more, in unexpected, unanticipated ways – and not just scientifically but imaginatively and spiritually.

For such reasons, Blake argues that the relationship human beings should seek with nature, is not one of managed exploitation, managed consumption, or even managed cooperation, but instead is one aimed at a kairos-type transformation. You begin to feel the difference by considering other aphorisms of his. They signal a way of seeing that is free from what closes the doors of perception.

A Robin Red breast in a Cage
Puts all Heaven in a Rage.
Each outcry of the hunted Hare
A fibre of the Brain does tear.
A Skylark wounded in the wing
A Cherubim does cease to sing.

If you read these lines not as painful moral injunctions but pointers towards a wider reality, you can feel your mind on the verge of change. They each attend to a poignant moment, hold its suffering, and contemplate its true extent. The finite knocks us to the infinite. The cruel captivity and needless slaughter are symptoms of ignorance, a lack of sight that can be remedied. Further, if someone really sees a world in a grain of sand, they simultaneously realize that the grain of sand is offering praise too. The observer and the observed, now lover and beloved, join hands and step towards becoming a new creation.

My sense is that an eternity-focused ecological education would radically extend the awareness of the ecologies of which we're a part, and make us be glad to know them, and so want them to flourish. Desire might drive economic change. Such sight could become part of the reopening of the cosmos in ways that the Praetorian guard would definitely frown on. This would embrace not just the evolved organisms studied by the natural sciences, but the divine intelligences that accompany them, as has been appreciated by mystics and visionaries. It would revisit the panoply of gods, spirits and daemons that our ancestors took as read, and wonder if we could know them again.

To regain serious contact with these dimensions of reality matters, not only because we are made to enjoy them, and so cutting them out is cutting off a part of ourselves: it frustrates our spiritual intelligence. It matters because the material world alone is clearly too small for us: we are Homo spiritualis, spirit-loving, meaning-discovering creatures. "More! More! is the cry of a mistaken soul, less than All cannot satisfy Man," Blake realized. That "All" is only satisfied by felt contact with what's immaterial and transcendent: the spiritual commons. We are supposed to grow into these other dimensions, not insist that a flattened reality satisfy our need for growth, which will clearly only deplete and exhaust things.

## Avoiding dystopias

These dimensions of existence are before us. The alternative learning and revivified spirit they could inspire might sustain the mental fight that will be required as we face the state we're in. And it is a mental fight. In a democracy, you can't force people to change. Even in a tyranny, compulsion is as likely to destroy as free, to recast as break people's chains. More subtle is the point made by many writers, from Plato to Ursula Le Guin, who have considered the siren attractions of utopias. Time and again, these writers have stressed that trying to build heaven on earth is fatal. When it is attempted, by revolutionaries or dictators, the world has proven itself too complex, the unexpected consequences too unpredictable, the people who were supposed to be helped too diverse. Utopian manifestoes are recipes for mass violence. Genuine renewal and rebirth require a challenge that reaches for much more than is currently known. It must speak to and activate what's languishing and lost, though innate and always ready: heaven is nearby, radiating through earthy troubles and faults. Mortal life can become open and transparent to heaven.

An answer to human affairs is not found in a single solution that can be imposed across the globe. It is found in multiple visions of a unified reality, that spiritual intelligence can appreciate in eternity. This is the approach of kairos – learning by perceiving, changing by loving, forgiving repeat mistakes, trusting in free, discerned imagining. Chronos doesn't much like it because its myth is not multidimensional but flat – the myth of measurable, demonstrable, material progress. It produces naively optimistic cheerleaders, who cite statistics and the latest theories, and demoralize people when the setbacks and disasters inevitably come. Eternity is needed because when things go wrong and people disagree, as they will, we might survive the resulting conflicts by recognizing that most opponents want what is good. GCtNLUG. There is a dimension in which we're connected.

Societies do, and have existed, by this spiritual light. The medieval European world was, in large part, built around the presence of kairos. I remember once standing on the Malvern Hills, overlooking Worcestershire, and spotting the remains of medieval monasteries and still-standing churches. My companion, who knew the area, pointed out that a person living at the time might never have been more than half an hour from a religious house, keeping the liturgy of the hours, even if they were travelling on foot. Different types of time coexisted. The world was more diverse, not forced into a monocrop existence. We can't go back and, of course, those times coexisted with exploitation and horrors, but the past is often a source of the most radical ideas for today because it highlights what exists and has been forgotten.

This is invaluable. In former ages, there was always the possibility of redemption. Only in a secular age can humanity experience itself as a failure, because its only project is itself. Apart from everything else we have explored in these pages, spiritual intelligence might be needed to experience the rest of the twenty-first century as other than a decline and fall. For there is a truth that can be known. Crises happen. But even when they appear grave and pointless, and to be escalating only suffering, they can be eucatastrophic. This is Tolkien's word. It describes the kairotic glimpse of truth that comes, though the whole of nature feels driven by a merciless chug of terrible, destructive events. He knew of despair. He was in the trenches of the First World War. And there he discovered what we are truly made for.

We are Homo spiritualis. Inner freedom is ours. Rich simplicity can be seen. The soul can settle. Death will prove a portal. The good remains committed. Kairos is waiting to break through in the slightest rustle and fall of leaves. This is our story, and it informs what to do and how to be. It emerges from the dark thick of things as "a sudden and miraculous power: never to be counted on to recur."[71] Only it does. It doesn't deny suffering and failure, but does deny, in the face of seeming evidence, any final defeat. It is "joy beyond the walls of the world, poignant as grief," Tolkien wrote. It is known with spiritual intelligence.

### *A final quote*
"The moment of greatest separation must be the moment of greatest awareness of that separation and therefore greatest

awareness of that from which you are separate." Verlyn Flieger, *Splintered Light*.

## *A final practice*

Imagine, for a moment, that there is no tomorrow. What difference does that make to your today?

# Notes

1. Cited by Kastrup, B. (2020). *Decoding Schopenhauer's Metaphysics*. London: Iff Books
2. Schrödinger, E. (1967). *What is Life?* Cambridge: Cambridge University Press, p. 87
3. Murdoch, I. (1971). *The Sovereignty of Good*. London: Routledge, p. 100
4. Retrieved from https://www.theguardian.com/commentis free/2021/mar/28/the-guardian-view-on-post-christian-brit ain-a-spiritual-enigma
5. Bellah, R. (2011). *Religion in Human Evolution: From the Paleolithic to the Axial Age*. London: Belknap Press, p. xv
6. I have written directly about the findings of the research here – https://aeon.co/essays/how-trance-states-forged-human-society-through-transcendence
7. Dunbar, R. et al. (2014). *Thinking Big: How the Evolution of Social Life Shaped the Human Mind*. London: Thames and Hudson, p. 80
8. Barker, G. (2009). *The Agricultural Revolution in Prehistory: Why did Foragers become Farmers?* Oxford: Oxford University Press, p. 409
9. Fuentes, A. (2019). *Why We Believe: Evolution and the Human Way of Being*. London: Yale University Press, p. xiii
10. ibid., p. 36
11. Schrödinger, ibid., p. 68
12. Harari, Y.N. (2011). *Sapiens: A Brief History of Humankind*. London: Vintage Books, p. 27
13. Bloch, M. (2008). *Why Religion Is Nothing Special But Is Central*. Retrieved from https://royalsocietypublishing.org/doi/10.1098/rstb.2008.0007#d3e176
14. Dunbar, ibid., p. 7
15. Martin, C.L. (1992). *In the Spirit of the Earth: Rethinking*

*History and Time.* Baltimore: The Johns Hopkins University Press, p. 45

16. Thompson, W.I. (1996). *The Time Falling Bodies Take To Light.* New York: St. Martin's Griffin, p. 127
17. Cauvin, J. (2000). *The Birth of the Gods and the Origins of Agriculture.* Cambridge: Cambridge University Press
18. Toynbee, A.J. (1946). *A Study of History: Abridgement of Volumes I-VI.* D.C. Somervell (ed). Oxford: Oxford University Press, p. 193
19. Bellah, ibid., p. 94
20. Parry explores these issues in his film, *Tawai*, as well as on his website, https://www.bruceparry.com/blog/pod/
21. Cited by Bellah, ibid., p. 205
22. ibid., p. 263
23. Jaspers, K. (1953). *The Origin and Goal of History.* New Haven: Yale University Press, p. 4
24. Taylor, C. (2012). "What Was the Axial Revolution?" in Bellah, R. and Joas, H. (eds). *The Axial Age and Its Consequences.* London: Belknap Press, p. 36
25. Toynbee, ibid., p. 227
26. ibid., p. 228
27. Aeschylus. (1959). "Prometheus Bound" in Grene, D. and Lattimore, R. (eds). *The Complete Greek Tragedies, Vol 1.* Chicago: University of Chicago Press, p. 327
28. Retrieved from https://lithub.com/on-the-yoruba-traditions-complex-philosophical-heritage/
29. Roetz, H. (2012). "The Axial Age Theory: A Challenge to Historicism or an Explanatory Device of Civilization Analysis? With a Look at the Normative Discourse in Axial Age China" in Bellah, R. and Joas, H. (eds). *The Axial Age and Its Consequences.* London: Belknap Press, p. 257
30. Jaspers, ibid., p. 219
31. Mill, J.S. (1989). *Autobiography.* London: Penguin Books, p. 121

32. From "Lines Composed a Few Miles above Tintern Abbey"

33. Julian of Norwich. (2015). *Revelations of Divine Love*. Windeatt, B. (trans). Oxford: Oxford University Press, p. 45

34. Retrieved from https://tricycle.org/magazine/ten-oxherding -pictures/

35. I am grateful to Bernardo Kastrup for these references, in *Decoding Schopenhauer's Metaphysics*, ibid.

36. Bergson, H. (1911). *Creative Evolution*. Mitchell, A. (trans). New York: Henry Holt and Company, p. 165

37. Atiyah made these remarks in a keynote speech entitled "Mathematics in the 20th Century".

38. Rowson, J. (2019). *The Moves that Matter: A Chess Grandmaster on the Game of Life*. London: Bloomsbury, p. 240

39. Cited by Cunningham, C. (2010). *Darwin's Pious Idea: Why the Ultra-Darwinists and Creationists Both Get It Wrong*. Grand Rapids, Michigan: William B. Eerdmans Publishing, p. 151

40. Murdoch, ibid., p. 100

41. Julian of Norwich, ibid., p. 47

42. Cited in Swan, L. (2016). *The Wisdom of the Beguines: The Forgotten Story of a Medieval Women's Movement*. New York: BlueBridge, p. 119

43. Retrieved from https://unherd.com/thepost/wellness-is-no-replacement-for-religion/

44. Jung, C. (1989). *Memories, Dreams, Reflections*. New York: Vintage Books, pp. 61-2

45. Grant Watson, E.L. (1992). *The Mystery of Physical Life*. Edinburgh: Floris Books, p. 60

46. ibid., p. 71

47. Meister Eckhart. Sermon IV. Retrieved from https://www. ccel.org/ccel/eckhart/sermons.vii.html

48. Gilchrist, A. *Life of William Blake*. Retrieved from https:// en.wikisource.org/wiki/Page:Life_of_William_Blake,_ Gilchrist.djvu/466

49. Kean, L. (2017). *Surviving Death*. New York: Three Rivers Press, p. 362

50. I've written more fully about Blake's fourfold imagination here, from which these paragraphs are drawn – https://aeon.co/essays/what-we-can-learn-from-william-blakes-visionary-imagination

51. Sklar, S. (2020). "William Blake's Mythic System". Temenos Academy online papers, 6

52. Julian of Norwich, ibid., p. 51

53. Murdoch, ibid., p. 58

54. Boyd, C.A. and Timpe, K. (2021). *The Virtues: A Very Short Introduction*. Oxford: Oxford University Press, p. 6

55. Retrieved from https://systems-souls-society.com/finding-virtue-in-the-virtual/

56. Aristotle. (2000). *Nicomachean Ethics*. Crisp, R. (trans). Cambridge: Cambridge University Press, p. 50

57. Retrieved from https://systems-souls-society.com/what-is-this-the-case-for-continually-questioning-our-online-experience/

58. Partington, M. (2012). *If You Sit Very Still*. Bristol: Vala Publishing, p. 132

59. ibid., p. 136

60. ibid., p. 137

61. Murdoch, ibid., p. 101

62. Barfield, O. (2012). *History, Guilt and Habit*. Oxford: Barfield Press, pp. 48-50

63. McGilchrist, I. (2009). *The Master and His Emissary*. London: Yale University Press, p. 336

64. Taylor, C. (2007). *A Secular Age*. London: Belknap Press, p. 54

65. Steiner, G. (1989). *Real Presences*. London: Faber and Faber, p. 226

66. Barfield, O. (1971). *What Coleridge Thought*. Middletown, Connecticut: Wesleyan University Press, p. 10

67. I have a transcript of this event, which was held at the Kettering Foundation in 1982, and have published a long summary of Bohm and Barfield's conversation here – https://www.markvernon.com/david-bohm-and-owen-barfield-a-conversation

68. Cited in Walter Isaacson. (2007). *Einstein: His Life And Universe*. London: Pocket Books, p. 549

69. Weil, S. (2009). *Waiting For God*. New York: Harper Perennial, p. 61

70. Retrieved from https://www.natureinstitute.org/article/craig-holdrege/goethe-and-the-evolution-of-science

71. Tolkien, J.R.R. (1966). "On Fairy-Stories" in *Essays Presented to Charles Williams*. Lewis, C.S. (ed). Grand Rapids, Michigan: William Eerdmans Publishing Company, p. 81

# Index

Hammurabi 52
happiness 76–77
Harari, Yuval Noah 29, 38–39, 47, 162
Hart, David Bentley 6
Hawaiian society 55–56
Hayward, Guy 12
Heidegger, Martin 172
Heisenberg, Werner 154–155
Hepworth, Barbara 198
Herzog, Werner 34–35
hierarchical societies 54–58
Hildegard of Bingen 84
Hinduism 125, 142, 199–200 *see also Bhagavad Gita; Upanishads*
Hobbes, Thomas 178
Hockney, David 198
Homo heidelbergensis 20–21, 30, 36–37
Homo neanderthalensis 20–25, 30, 35, 36, 37
Homo sapiens 16–17, 19, 30–36, 37–42
Homo spiritualis 17, 41–42, 211, 213
hormones 162
human-animal hybrids 34, 39
human evolution 16–42
    awareness of the absent and invisible 22–24
    egalitarian societies 45–47, 88–89
    hierarchical societies 54–58
    Homo sapiens as Homo

spiritualis 16–17, 41–42, 211, 213
    individuality, emergence of 54–56, 58–61, 63, 66–71, 87–89
    intentionality 19–22, 30–32
    lever technology 48–50
    meaning-discovery 28–30
    niche-discovery 24–28
    ritual, importance of 17–19
    settling and farming 37–41
    spiritual technologies 35–37
    transcendence 32–35
    uniformitarianism, the myth of 44–45, 65
    virtue and 159–162
human sacrifices 56–57, 177–178
Hume, David 166, 178
humility 180–181
hunter-gatherer societies, contemporary *see* indigenous peoples

Iamblichus 118–119
Ibn 'Arabi 85–86, 123–125
identity politics 172–176
Ignatius Loyola 167–168
Illich, Ivan 155, 196
imagination 80–81, 130, 204
improvisation, expanding awareness through 11–12
India, ancient 67–68
indigenous peoples

on Atlantis 87–88

on the city state 65, 184

dialogical qualities 205

divided line analogy 96, 130

*Phaedo* (death of Socrates) 132–142

on silence 97

on virtues 164

Plutarch 195

Polkinghorne, John 188

popular culture 9–10

Porete, Marguerite 91, 152

postmortem existence 127–128, 130–131

Prometheus, story of 63–64

prophets 58, 60, 62, 94–95, 198

psychotherapy 12, 135, 163–164, 176, 207–208

radical empiricism 135, 141, 150

reality 96–99

reductionism 90–91, 121, 154–155

religion

in Ancient Egypt 48, 50

death, relationship to life 142–143

emergence of 47–48

ritual and 17–19, 23, 199–200

soul work and 110–111, 113–114

spiritual intelligence and 8–9

*see also individual faiths and religious figures*

ritual 17–19, 23, 32–33, 36–37, 46, 199–200

Roetz, Heiner 68

Rowson, Jonathan 98

Saadi 2

sacred places 38

sacrifice

animal and human 56–57, 177–178

self- 148–153, 161, 197

Salami, Minna 65–66

Schopenhauer, Arthur 3, 88

Schrödinger, Erwin 3–4, 26

science

evolutionary psychology and virtue 159–162

intuited truth and 188–189

kairos shifts in knowledge 202–204

methodology 81

objective truth 101

purpose of, compared with myth and ritual 29–30

reductionism 90–91, 121, 154–155

simplicity and 91–93

soulful discovery 119–122

second self 107–108

self-sacrifice 148–153, 161, 197

selfhood 86–89

settlement, origins of human

# ACADEMIC AND SPECIALIST

### Why Materialism Is Baloney
How true skeptics know there is no death and fathom answers to life, the universe, and everything
Bernardo Kastrup
A hard-nosed, logical, and skeptic non-materialist metaphysics, according to which the body is in mind, not mind in the body.
Paperback: 978-1-78279-362-5 ebook: 978-1-78279-361-8

### The Fall
Steve Taylor
*The Fall* discusses human achievement versus the issues of war, patriarchy and social inequality.
Paperback: 978-1-78535-804-3 ebook: 978-1-78535-805-0

### Brief Peeks Beyond
Critical essays on metaphysics, neuroscience, free will, skepticism and culture
Bernardo Kastrup
An incisive, original, compelling alternative to current mainstream cultural views and assumptions.
Paperback: 978-1-78535-018-4 ebook: 978-1-78535-019-1

## Framespotting
Changing how you look at things changes how
you see them
Laurence & Alison Matthews
A punchy, upbeat guide to framespotting. Spot deceptions and
hidden assumptions; swap growth for growing up. See and be free.
Paperback: 978-1-78279-689-3 ebook: 978-1-78279-822-4

## Is There an Afterlife?
David Fontana
Is there an Afterlife? If so what is it like? How do Western ideas
of the afterlife compare with Eastern? David Fontana presents the
historical and contemporary evidence for survival of
physical death.
Paperback: 978-1-90381-690-5

## Nothing Matters
a book about nothing
Ronald Green
Thinking about Nothing opens the world to everything by
illuminating new angles to old problems and stimulating new
ways of thinking.
Paperback: 978-1-84694-707-0 ebook: 978-1-78099-016-3

## Panpsychism
The Philosophy of the Sensuous Cosmos
Peter Ells
Are free will and mind chimeras? This book, anti-materialistic but
respecting science, answers: No! Mind is foundational
to all existence.
Paperback: 978-1-84694-505-2 ebook: 978-1-78099-018-7

**Punk Science**
Inside the Mind of God
Manjir Samanta-Laughton
Many have experienced unexplainable phenomena; God, psychic abilities, extraordinary healing and angelic encounters. Can cutting-edge science actually explain phenomena previously thought of as 'paranormal'?
Paperback: 978-1-90504-793-2

**The Vagabond Spirit of Poetry**
Edward Clarke
Spend time with the wisest poets of the modern age and of the past, and let Edward Clarke remind you of the importance of poetry in our industrialized world.
Paperback: 978-1-78279-370-0 ebook: 978-1-78279-369-4

Readers of ebooks can buy or view any of these bestsellers by clicking on the live link in the title. Most titles are published in paperback and as an ebook. Paperbacks are available in traditional bookshops. Both print and ebook formats are available online. Find more titles and sign up to our readers' newsletter at
http://www.johnhuntpublishing.com/non-fiction
Follow us on Facebook at
https://www.facebook.com/JHPNonFiction
and Twitter at https://twitter.com/JHPNonFiction